Automating Library Acquisitions

Issues and Outlook

by
Richard W. Boss

Knowledge Industry Publications, Inc.
White Plains, NY and London

Professional Librarian Series

Automating Library Acquisitions: Issues and Outlook

Library of Congress Cataloging in Publication Data

Boss, Richard W.
    Automating library acquisitions, issues and
outlook.

    (Professional librarian series)
    Bibliography: p.
    Includes index.
    1. Acquisitions (Libraries)--Automation.
I. Title.   II. Series.
Z689.B74   1982   025.2'028'54   82-8941
ISBN 0-86729-006-4 (pbk.)   AACR2

Printed in the United States of America

10   9   8   7   6   5   4   3   2   1

Table of Contents

Preface

The automation of acquisitions procedures has become the most active area of library automation, with more than 20 organizations offering automated acquisitions systems as of early 1982—more options than there were available for the automation of any other library function. The plethora of choices appeared to reflect the needs of vendors more than the needs of libraries. Major bibliographic utilities (OCLC, RLIN and UTLAS) wished to extend their shared cataloging systems; turnkey system vendors (CLSI, DataPhase, Geac, etc.) wished to augment their circulation control systems to include related functions; book wholesalers wished to promote online ordering to reduce their order fulfillment costs and to promote book sales.

The acquisitions operation encompasses the selection, ordering, claiming, receipt, payment and accounting of library materials. It has not been easy to automate acquisitions because libraries' requirements in this area vary more than they do in cataloging or circulation. Both of the latter functions are substantially under the control of librarians, but acquisitions involves purchasing and financial policies and procedures that are usually controlled by another unit within the library's parent organization. The problems of designing automated acquisitions systems that could be used by any library were substantially overcome by early 1982, primarily by developing systems which offered a range of purchase order and financial report formats. As these design considerations were mastered, it became increasingly apparent that a library considering the automation of acquisitions had to address a number of issues, including the relationship of automated acquisitions to other automated library functions, priorities among system features, cost, ease of adoption and termination, and vendor reliability. This book identifies and describes these issues.

1
Issues in Automating Acquisitions

The primary motives that will prompt libraries to investigate automated acquisitions systems in the 1980s appear to be the hope of realizing cost reduction or cost containment, speeding the receipt of materials, improving fund control, expanding single function systems into integrated systems and being in the forefront of librarianship.

Nevertheless, the major initiative in automating acquisitions appears to be coming from the vendors of automated library systems, both commercial and noncommercial. The bibliographic utilities and turnkey circulation system vendors have substantially completed the development of software for their initial products and are seeking to broaden their range of services. Book wholesalers with in-house computer systems see significant financial benefits from having libraries submit orders online.

Circumstances have changed dramatically since the 1960s when most libraries first became aware of the potential of acquisitions automation. Twenty years ago the library's greatest concern was ordering. Acquisitions funds were somewhat more plentiful than today and libraries were often pressed to spend all of their money before the end of the fiscal year.

Twenty years ago the cost of full-size or mainframe computers was so high that few libraries considering automation could afford to obtain their own computers; most had to rely on sharing a large full-size computer with other departments in their organization. In this climate there were two options for automating acquisitions: develop the system in-house or transfer the software developed by another library. Developing software in-house was extremely expensive, and purchasing software from another library was extremely difficult because the programming languages in use at that time were very hardware specific and therefore difficult to transfer or "transport" from computer to computer.

At the beginning of the 1980s, the concerns of the acquisitions librarian are no longer primarily associated with ordering, but with collection development and sound management of funds. The problem for most libraries is how to make the best collection development decisions in light of scarce resources and the mission and goals of the parent organization. It has frequently been said that the most significant part of acquisitions work—that which involves the planned selection of materials, both new and old, best calculated to strengthen the institution's resources—takes place before the books are actually ordered. Modern acquisitions systems are increasingly expected to do more than provide purchase order writing, accurate outstanding order information, timely reports and good funds control. They must also become tools for selectors by providing detailed collection information.

The early acquisitions systems were tied to expensive full-size computers. The dramatic hardware developments of the 1970s have now made it possible for almost any library, even one with a limited budget, to consider an online system. Full-size computers are more powerful and less expensive than ever before. Minicomputers and microcomputers offer more limited, but considerable, processing power at even lower cost. Twenty years ago a minimum investment in automated system hardware was over $1 million; today it is less than $15,000.

The options for automating acquisitions now include not only in-house development, but also the purchase of a system or services from a vendor. The number of vendor options had grown to at least twenty automated acquisitions systems or subsystems by early 1982. For the first time the offerings of the major bibliographic utilities (OCLC, RLIN and UTLAS) duplicate those of the vendors of turnkey stand-alone systems (CLSI, Data-Phase, Geac, etc.). A turnkey system is one that includes, in a single procurement, all hardware, software, installation, training, hardware/software maintenance and software enhancement. In addition, wholesalers with established bookselling relationships with libraries are offering systems, and some companies previously not associated with libraries are entering the field.

The number of choices appears overwhelming at first, especially to someone who does not regard him/herself as an expert in library automation. The natural tendency is to rely on "experts" to make a recommendation. Yet many of the issues that must be addressed are not of a technological nature. A librarian may unintentionally abdicate important judgments to someone with a more limited, less informed perspective.

Among the issues which must be addressed are:

A. *Integration or connection with other automated functions*—Given the large number of sources for the automation of acquisitions, how can the library coordinate the automation of this function with the automation of other library functions?

B. *Features*—What is the relative importance of each of the following to the library:
   1) Data base access
   2) Name/address file
   3) Purchase order writing
   4) Online ordering
   5) In-process file
   6) Claiming

7) Receiving/paying
8) Funds accounting
9) Management information
10) Vendor monitoring

C. *Cost over time*—What is the projected cost of the automated system over a period of time (generally calculated for five years), including both capital and operating expenses?

D. *Ease of adoption and cancellation*—How easy will it be to adopt the system and how easily could the library discontinue the system if it did not work well or if a more attractive option became available?

E. *Vendor reliability*—Does the vendor of the system have the financial resources to continue to support it, and have its previous customers been satisfied with its performance?

Each of these issues will be discussed in this book.

HISTORY OF AUTOMATED ACQUISITIONS

Librarians have been thinking and writing about library automation for at least four decades. Ralph Parker was working on the implementation of library automation during the 1930s at the University of Texas. The automation of acquisitions and circulation was contemplated, but it was nearly 20 years after the first experimental automated circulation system before both activities were, in fact, automated. The Montclair (NJ) Public Library adopted a punched-card circulation system in 1941 after several years of investigation. The library staff at the University of Illinois, Circle Campus, was aware of the potential of automation from the very founding of the library in 1947, although it again took a number of years to implement a plan. In his first annual report the librarian stated:

> Thought has also been given to the possibility of making use of the undergraduate division's extensive installation of IBM punched card equipment in the book order procedures and it is not at all unlikely that some application of this sort will eventually be undertaken.[1]

Early Library Automation

Acquisitions operations were a popular target for the application of automation during the first growth period of library automation: the late 1950s through 1970. Hundreds of libraries automated their procedures for the ordering, receipt and payment of library materials. The early systems tended to be order/receipt control systems or funds accounting systems. Only a few combined the two functions. Virtually all of the development was done in-house on equipment owned by the libraries' parent organizations.

As long ago as 1957, the University of Missouri Library was printing its purchase orders using punched-card equipment. Within a few years several other large academic and public libraries were punching Hollerith cards and feeding order information into computers to print purchase orders. The Brown, Harvard and Yale University libraries were among the first to automate order/receipt control.

Automation was also applied to claiming. By the mid-1960s, the University of Michigan had a system that printed claim notices on overdue orders at monthly intervals. The system provided for specification of the period after which any particular order was to be regarded as overdue—e.g., the period might be longer for orders sent overseas than for domestic orders. The system also printed lists of exceptional orders—such as those for which three claim notices had been issued—for detailed investigation. The Michigan system was among the most popular for transfer to other libraries that wished to avoid the expense of developing their own programs for acquisitions automation. The University of Utah Library was one which sought to adopt the Michigan system. However, the programs of the day were highly machine-dependent, and even though both universities had Univac 1108 computers the programs had to be extensively rewritten before they could be transferred.

Funds accounting systems were popular because many of the libraries' parent institutions were providing financial information in formats that were not useful to the libraries. Monthly reports of encumbrances and expenditures were not available until two to four weeks after the close of the month, and they summarized information by purchase order number without identifying the individual items ordered or the unit of the library for which they were acquired. Libraries, therefore, sought to develop more timely and detailed reports.

Growth of Acquisitions Automation

More sophisticated acquisitions automation began in the mid-1960s—a period of rapid growth for many institutions. At the time, the author was the acquisitions librarian at a major academic research library where the acquisitions budget grew by 350% over a six-year period. Such growth was common to a number of libraries and emphasized the need to increase staff productivity. Some of the automated acquisitions systems developed at this time sought to address ordering and funds accounting. While still produced in-house, the systems were able to control the various aspects of ordering: producing purchase orders; issuing open order reports; printing in-process reports; and summarizing expenditures by purchase order, vendor, unit of the library or requestor. The greatest drawback was that the systems operated in batch mode. The data were periodically fed into the computer and were output solely in hard-copy form at fixed intervals.

The mid-1960s was also the period of blanket order development. A number of libraries, primarily in academic institutions, began to place orders with jobbers to automatically supply all research level material produced by major publishers. The libraries were thus relieved of much of the paperwork of ordering. But the two solutions for improving library productivity were often in conflict. The automated systems were developed by librarians, while blanket ordering procedures were developed by book wholesalers. Some libraries that were producing individual purchase orders by computer were once again forced to revert to manual methods because they could not find an effective way to use the computer to handle the blanket orders which represented an increasingly larger percentage of total acquisitions.

While some comprehensive systems were developed, a majority of the systems started before the late 1970s did not automate all acquisitions functions because of the serious limitations—technical, financial and political—on the libraries that developed them. A market, therefore, existed for comprehensive vendor-produced systems for which the developmental costs could be spread among a number of library clients.

Development of Vendor-supplied Systems

The first vendor-supplied system was a batch software package called BATAB, a product of North America's largest book wholesaler, Baker & Taylor (B&T). The system was first made available in 1969 and was purchased by more than four dozen libraries, which mounted it on their local full-size computers. The system, although still used by several libraries, is no longer supported. During the eight years that B&T actively marketed BATAB it was the most comprehensive commercially developed system available, offering selection lists, purchase orders, multiple-part order sets, open order reports, in-process reports, detailed funds accounting, invoice clearing, the capacity to detect problem invoices, claim and cancellation notices, vendor lists, statistics, and various exception and historical reports.

In 1972 a new company, CLSI, introduced an online minicomputer-based acquisitions system. The system featured creation and printing of purchase orders, on-order/in-process control, accounting, etc. At least nine systems were sold before the company changed its focus to circulation control (when it discovered that acquisitions automation was extremely difficult to standardize because each library wanted different purchase order formats and accounting procedures).

The next vendor-supplied system was IROS (Instant Response Order System), an online ordering system developed by Brodart, a major book jobber, in 1978. The system allowed libraries to access Brodart's files to determine what titles were available and to place orders online. Users only needed a computer terminal and a modem to access the system, but its range of function was limited, excluding such operations as open order control, in-process files, funds accounting, etc.

The Washington Library Network (WLN), a regional bibliographic utility, was the first utility to offer an acquisitions system. Introduced in 1978, the system provides a full range of ordering and accounting functions.

By the late 1970s, as the number of vendor-supported systems grew, many of the in-house systems in use in libraries were more than a decade old. Almost all of them were batch systems, developed for full-size computers available to the libraries. Batch systems are those in which data are stock-piled and only periodically fed into the computer, which is almost always a full-size computer outside the library. Punched cards or magnetic tape are the most common forms of input; output is usually a printout. Batch systems normally have response times measured in days and are almost always limited to single functions. In contrast, online systems, such as those developed by Brodart and WLN, measure response times in seconds and can handle many related functions concurrently. There was, therefore, a gradual movement from batch to online systems in the late 1970s, with a majority of the libraries adopting vendor produced systems.

Approximately one out of five libraries with annual acquisitions budgets of more than $200,000 were using an automated acquisitions system by late 1981.[2] The most common systems in use were the online ordering systems of the major book wholesalers: Baker and Taylor's LIBRIS and Brodart's OLAS (the successor to IROS). Nearly 100 libraries were using these systems, the majority of them large public libraries. The second most common approach to automating acquisitions was the use of in-house systems, most of them batch systems installed in the late 1960s and early 1970s. Most of the 60 in-house systems that could be identified were in academic libraries. The smallest, but fastest growing segment was of bibliographic utility systems. Approximately 15 libraries were using the Washington Library Network's system, the oldest comprehensive online acquisitions system developed for use in a multi-library environment. Another 20 libraries were using the OCLC (Online Computer Library Center) acquisitions system released in late 1981 and more than 30 other libraries had placed orders for it. Eleven Research Library Information Network (RLIN) users had committed themselves to use that utility's acquisitions system, still under development in 1981.

THE MOTIVATION

Before a library begins the process of developing or selecting an automated acquisitions system, library administration should examine its motivation in undertaking the activity. This is not to suggest that there are good or bad reasons for automating, but there must be a clearly stated rationale to the process, so that the many decisions which must be made can be made quickly and consistently. Common motivations include:

1) Reducing ordering backlogs
2) Reducing acquisitions costs
3) Containing acquisitions costs
4) Speeding order writing and/or receipt of materials
5) Improving funds control
6) Expanding a single function automated system into an integrated system
7) Improving management information
8) Achieving compatability with resource sharing partners
9) Committing the library to the use of technology

The motivation may be to seek a solution to an existing problem, to anticipate a prospective problem, or merely a wish to do something perceived to be more efficient. It is imperative that the administration of the library be very honest with itself in determining its motivation, even if it should decide not to share its reasoning with others. An objective study of the options may lead to a decision not to automate. Library automation consultants are often told that library administration wishes to automate to achieve a specified objective. When the consultant determines that the objective cannot be achieved through automation, the library administration concludes that automation will, nevertheless, be undertaken—sometimes for the originally stated reasons and sometimes for other reasons. If the motivation is a desire to automate because of a belief that automation is the modern way of administering a library, the library administrators should acknowledge this, at least among themselves.

The motivation of the library director is very important in the automation project. In more than 150 telephone interviews conducted by the author and his associates in 1981, the library director was identified by virtually all interviewees as the principal decision maker in an automation commitment. The decision to automate is apparently deemed to be one of the most important developments in a library, and directors choose to reserve the major role for themselves. The decision-making process appeared to be a source of irritation for many of the non-administrators interviewed.

The author, therefore, talked with 80 library directors to determine why they might automate acquisitions. Each director was asked whether acquisitions might be automated within the next five years, and if so why? More than 75% responded that they expected to automate the function. Almost all of the nearly 25% who did not expect to automate acquisitions cited lack of funds as the principal reason for not doing so. Only four directors said that they saw no reason to automate because the manual systems were adequate. The comments of the directors are incorporated into the balance of this chapter.

Reducing Ordering Backlogs

Automation almost always speeds the rate at which work is performed by relieving the staff of repetitive chores, improving the accuracy and integrity of files, eliminating the multiple entry of data, and facilitating the reformatting of data to accommodate changing needs.

The reduction of ordering backlogs was once a major motivation for automating, but it was cited by only two of 80 directors interviewed. Half of the directors interviewed said that problems of backlogs had been solved by declines in their libraries' purchasing power—they are buying less than in the past and there is little prospect for a change for the better.

Some libraries have been forced to reduce staff or freeze positions, and have had ordering backlogs develop for that reason. Often, the personnel retrenchments have been matched or exceeded by retrenchments in other areas. Therefore, there is no money to commit to automate the function.

Reducing Costs

One of the most frequently cited reasons for considering automation of acquisitions is the hope of reducing the cost of ordering and paying for library materials. The majority of the directors interviewed mentioned this as their principal interest.

The cost-effectiveness of automation in libraries has not been clearly established, however. Libraries have very large bibliographic files, often consisting of hundreds of thousands of records. Only a small percentage of a file will be consulted in a given day—Becker and Hayes estimate as little as 0.1%.[3] This is in sharp contrast to the activity in most business organizations, where smaller files may be consulted a hundred times as frequently each day. Therefore, libraries cannot spread the cost of creating and maintaining a large data base over very many units of activity, as can typical businesses.

It has been argued that automated cataloging using OCLC or one of the other bibliographic utilities has saved libraries a great deal of money. In the author's view it is not automation alone that has produced the great cost savings reported; rather, it is the effect of access to a rich, shared bibliographic data base that in many libraries has reduced the percentage of costly original cataloging (typically from $17 to $40 per title) to less than 10% of total cataloging. The ability to create records and edit copy without retyping would be extremely expensive if that were the only effect of using a bibliographic utility.

It is extremely difficult to acquire just enough computer capability to speed up work done manually without also acquiring capabilities that far exceed the minimal needs. Since many of these "extra" features are highly desirable, libraries tend to use them. The cost of performing a single task may be reduced, but total operating costs may rise because more work is being done. An example of this is the additional work that flows from the availability of collection use statistics produced by an automated circulation system. It results in more weeding of little used materials, more purchases of replacement and added copies, and changes in collection development patterns. One might argue that these are all things that libraries should do all of the time, but in fact automation often stimulates libraries to undertake these previously neglected tasks.

Directors of large public libraries who are responsible for purchasing large numbers of copies for several branches are the most optimistic about cost reduction. The costs of acquisitions of this type can be extremely high because of extensive bookkeeping requirements. Strikingly, of those who had automated circulation in the past five years, none thought cost reduction could be achieved by the automation of any library function because none had realized cost savings by implementing an automated circulation system. However, virtually all of these directors reported dramatic improvements in service from such installations.

While there is little evidence that any library has reduced the cost of acquisitions by automating, the future prospects for cost-effective automated library systems are quite good. Hardware costs are decreasing and the unit cost of each transaction will be lower when several functions can share computer hardware and the data base. This concept is discussed at greater length in Chapter 6.

If cost reduction is a primary objective, current non-automated system costs should be determined, and this will probably require a cost study. A good study is time consuming and expensive. There is no point to undertaking all this work if cost reduction isn't the motive for automating. If it is, the cost study should be undertaken and the library administration should abide by the results. If it isn't, the cost study should be foregone and the library should concentrate on determining whether the other improvements sought will be realized. There are few good studies available to use as models, but an effective cost study should meet the criteria spelled out in Appendix I.

Containing Costs

Many of those who are skeptical about cost reduction nevertheless believe that costs can be contained. While a little over half the library directors interviewed thought automation would reduce costs, nearly all thought it would contain costs. It is recognized that while capital investment in automation may take several years to recover, once the system is installed it can usually absorb additional work at little increased cost. Usually, the unit cost of additional work drops. This has been confirmed in many libraries with automated systems.

More and more directors are citing cost containment, rather than cost reduction, as the reason for considering automation. Several said they had previously held the view that cost reductions could be achieved, but their own experience and that of others persuaded them that cost containment was a more realistic objective. If one does opt to automate with cost containment in mind, one should be able to determine current costs and project the rate of increase in those costs. This requires adequate historical cost information— something most libraries lack. Here again, a library should undertake a cost study which complies with the criteria described in Appendix I. The major categories of costs should then be projected, based on inflation and on prospective increases in activity.

A less expensive cost study could be undertaken by comparing the added cost of increasing (by some percentage) the level of acquisitions using existing procedures, with the cost of increasing (by the same percentage) the activity level using the automated system. That will not answer the question of whether the implementation cost of the automated system is recovered; it will only compare the capacity and cost of each to accommodate increased activity.

Speeding Order Writing and Receipt of Material

Library directors generally agree that automation will increase the speed of writing orders and receiving materials. This is particularly important to the directors of public libraries who are concerned that new books reach the shelves before reviews appear in news media or authors appear on television interview programs.

Several of the interviewees said that automating order writing got the orders to the vendors more quickly, but did little to improve the total time required to get materials. Reducing the order preparation process by a few days matters little if the vendor takes several weeks to supply the titles. Libraries experienced with wholesaler systems that transmit orders online to the vendor supplying the system and transmit printed orders to other vendors, found the following: getting the order to the vendor in machine-readable form (for direct entry into the vendor's order-fulfillment system) resulted in dramatic improvements in delivery time; however, the rapid production and mailing of printed orders for other vendors appeared to have no effect.

A few directors of special libraries (most of them libraries which order fewer than 2000 titles a year) who have had experience with automated systems said that while they liked the overall control the system provided, the total process had become more complex. One reported that automated systems which call for detailed input of data can actually increase the time required to prepare orders. Another said that a good manual system can produce purchase orders more quickly, and without creating backlogs. It is in the subsequent filing and retrieving of information and financial control that most benefits accrue from the automation of the function.

Improving Funds Control

Acquisitions consumes a large part of every library's budget and the pressures to account for expenditures are greater than ever. Most libraries have more than one fund from which purchases are made and a majority allocate the available funds among collections, departments or disciplines.

All of the directors interviewed consider improved funds control a major reason for automating acquisitions. Among the directors of large libraries it is the most important reason for considering automation.

It is imperative that the automated system be flexible enough to permit the setting up of accounts in the manner prescribed by the financial authorities in the library's parent institution. It should not be necessary to rewrite the reports from the automated acquisitions system into the formats required by the institution's accounting department. This requirement appears to have been the major reason for many libraries choosing to develop in-house acquisitions systems.

Expanding a Single Function System into an Integrated One

Over 3000 libraries have now had some experience with automation—shared cataloging, online circulation control or the searching of remote bibliographic data bases. They are, therefore, prepared to consider the automation of other library functions to create integrated systems, and modern computer hardware is capable of supporting the integration of several functions.

For most libraries cataloging and circulation control are the most important candidates for automation. Several automation options had been available for each of these functions for at least three years before viable automated acquisitions systems options began to appear. For many libraries the automation of acquisitions is, therefore, an augmentation of an existing system or systems.

The library directors interviewed want to be able to create a bibliographic record when an item is selected and to use the same record in the cataloging, circulation control and patron access catalog functions. Even when the automation of acquisitions is not cost effective in itself, it can be justified as an essential component of the overall automation program.

Improving Management Information

Automated systems can produce a substantial amount of management information, including detailed information about the relative cost of materials in various disciplines, vendor performance, etc. The library directors interviewed ranked improved management information as a high priority, but few were accustomed to using extensive management information in their work.

Unfortunately most automated systems produce more management information than an administrator can readily use. Few systems are designed to provide only "exceptional" information—for example, reporting the vendors who exceed a particular delivery time rather than producing detailed reports of how long it takes each vendor to deliver the average order.

One of the most important pieces of information in improving collection development is knowing how much the existing collection is used. The persons charged with selection should have access to information on patterns of use as one element in shaping their collection development programs. They should also be alerted when a large number of reserves or holds are placed against a title so that additional copies may be ordered.

Ideally, titles which are on order should be included in the circulation control system or patron access catalog so that reserves or holds can be checked against them and additional copies of high-demand titles ordered even before the initial order is met.

Achieving Compatibility with Resource-sharing Partners

More and more libraries are coordinating their acquisitions with other libraries. By sharing an automated system they can determine what is in each cooperating library's collection and what each has on order, thus avoiding unnecessary duplication.

A few of the library directors interviewed were already sharing automated circulation systems. Some were entering titles on order into their circulation systems before they were received so that the information could be shared.

Committing the Library to the Use of Technology

Nearly every technological advance in the past 100 years has excited the imagination of one librarian or another, and many advances have eventually been adopted by libraries. One example is the typewriter. It was in 1877, during the Conference of Librarians in New York, that the typewriter was mentioned as a possible tool for cataloging. In 1885 the typewriter was discussed at the Conference of Librarians at Lake George. Some of the librarians present had been trying different makes and models, and were convinced that the typewriter was a superior way of making catalog cards. However, there was still some question about the permanency of the ink. Those who went ahead had no proof that the ink was suitable, but they took a chance and introduced what was to become one of the most important technologies ever adopted by libraries.

The first articles in the literature explaining potential library applications of Hollerith punched cards, which were first used in the census of 1890, began to appear in the 1930s. As previously noted, the first experimental library automation was undertaken at the University of Texas in the mid-1930s; five years later the circulation system of the Montclair Public Library was changed to a punched-card machine installation. During this same period University of Florida Library staff members wrote about their experiences with a mechanized circulation system. While none of this early automation was cost- or service-effective, it laid the groundwork for the successful automated circulation efforts of later years.

By early 1982 online circulation control had matured as an application, with comprehensive systems containing nearly identical features available from several vendors. Comprehensive online acquisitions systems supported by vendors were still in their infancy. Some of those who chose to automate acquisitions sought to solve specific problems with their manual systems; others moved ahead because they were committed to a philosophy of employing new technology to improve library operations. This faith in technology has often been warranted, as it was in the case of the typewriter. It has also often led to failure—as it did with many of the dial access learning systems that were installed in the late 1960s.

There is a risk involved in automating acquisitions before all of the options are fully developed and can be observed in operation in libraries. It is extremely difficult to predict which of the vendors will offer the most comprehensive and cost-effective systems. There are, nevertheless, a number of librarians prepared to take the risk.

2

Acquisitions Functions

"Acquisitions," now more commonly used than the term "ordering," encompasses all aspects of the process of obtaining materials for libraries, including the location of information about materials to be ordered, receiving of materials, and the keeping of management information on procurement activities. The acquisition of all types of materials is normally included: monographs, serials, documents, microforms, maps, music scores and audiovisual materials. Acquisitions includes obtaining materials by purchase, gift or exchange. In some libraries the acquisitions process encompasses the selection of materials. Large libraries usually have separate acquisitions departments. In some cases the function is separated into monographs acquisition, serials, and exchange and gift units. In small libraries the responsibility may be assigned to a technical services division or may be kept under the direct control of the head librarian.

THE ACQUISITIONS PROCESS

Selection

The library acquisitions process starts with a selection by the acquisitions head, or with the arrival of a request for purchase from a designated selector. (Figure 2.1 outlines the acquisitions process.) The selector may be a collection development specialist, a librarian with responsibility for a particular collection or—in an academic institution—a faculty member. Many libraries encourage those who participate in book selection to record their suggestions on request slips. The use of a request slip has a number of benefits:

1) Participation in selection can be encouraged by distributing selection forms.
2) The structured format prompts the requesters to supply the information necessary for ordering.
3) Requests can more easily be processed if they are in a standard format.
4) The results of acquisitions checking and verification can be recorded on the form and returned to the requester if the material is already in the library or on order.
5) The forms can be used in various files and can later be returned to the requester to indicate that the item has been received and is ready for use.

15

Figure 2.1   The Steps Involved in Acquisitions

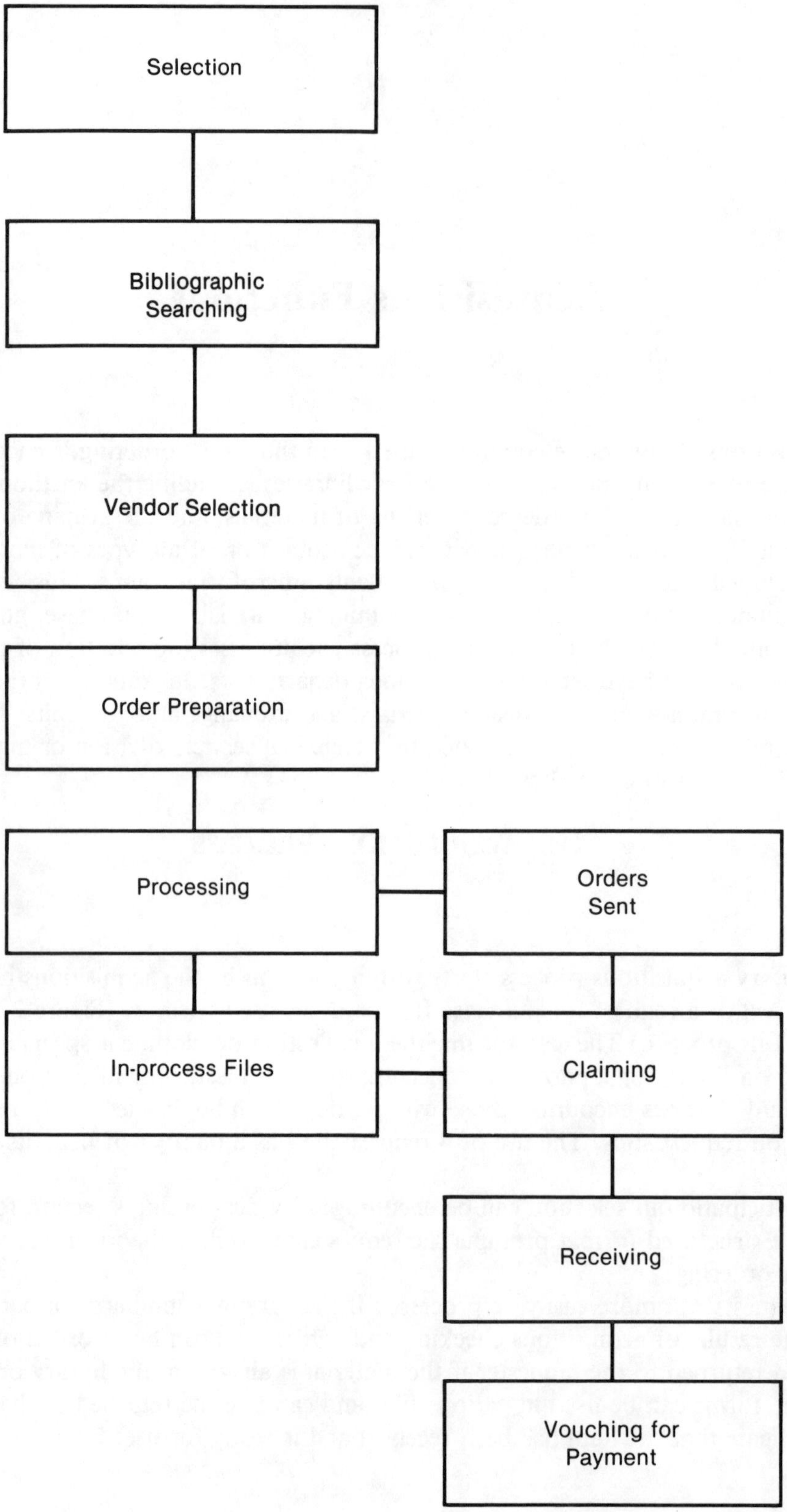

Verification

Many sources of information available to selectors do not include full details such as the purchase price or publisher's address. Determining the price and the publisher's address —if the order is to be sent direct—are aspects of pre-order searching or verification that make it possible for the order to be sent. Other aspects of verification are the correction of errors in the citation to prevent unwanted duplication and the obtaining of sufficient information to permit an order to be placed. In many libraries verification also provides information that will later be useful in cataloging, such as the correct form of the author's name and the Library of Congress card number.

Every library maintains a file of outstanding orders and larger libraries may have several. If the file is small it may contain not only items on order, but also items in-process. There will be cross references to the standing order file which is usually in a different format to allow the recording of multiple receipts on a single card. Some libraries maintain separate files for standing orders, approval plans, serials and documents.

Large libraries usually maintain many standing orders for series or even for all titles produced by a publisher of outstanding reputation. It is essential that these standing order files be checked prior to ordering to avoid duplicating by a firm order, that which is already scheduled to be received on standing order.

Normally everything is checked in the catalog before it is ordered, even materials which are usually not given full cataloging because inadvertent duplicates are unwanted. Some libraries temporarily file copies of outstanding orders and in-process slips in their catalogs to avoid separate checking of outstanding order files and the catalog. In a large library, however, cards for material on order or in process will probably be found more quickly in an outstanding order file than in a complex catalog.

These steps are not uniformly performed in this sequence. If the information on a request slip appears seriously deficient, bibliographic verification may be undertaken prior to the check against the catalog. Most verification can be eliminated if the item requested has a recent publication date, and is put out by a major trade publisher which publishes few series and is not on standing order.

Vendor Selection

After requests have been verified, the next major step is selecting the vendor from which the material is to be ordered. Some libraries order most of their books directly from publishers, but most libraries find that the time expended preparing separate orders, unpacking many small shipments and handling a large number of invoices is too great. Therefore, they consolidate most of their orders and place them with a wholesaler or jobber. Small libraries may have only two wholesalers; one each for monographs and serials. Large libraries often use different wholesalers for acquisitions from various parts of the world. Many wholesalers extend discounts for trade books and apply service charges for books which are given limited discount by the publisher. Serials wholesalers usually impose a service charge. A library's ordering volume may affect the discount schedule.

In addition to using one or more wholesalers, libraries frequently order from dealers who specialize in out-of-print materials. These are usually ordered after reviewing dealer catalogs. Rapid processing of such orders is necessary because there may be only a single copy available for most of the items in the catalog.

Order Preparation and Processing

Most libraries must establish their acquisitions routines within the regulations and procedures set by their parent institutions. For example, some organizations require that all orders be placed on full-sized purchase orders rather than on the three-inch by five-inch forms favored by most libraries and wholesalers. Most libraries use multiple-copy order forms. One copy is sent to the vendor (a wholesaler or a publisher) as an order; a second copy may be sent to the vendor to be used as a report if the item is unavailable; another copy is filed alphabetically by main entry or title in the library's outstanding order file; and an additional copy may be filed by purchase order number to facilitate claiming of long-outstanding orders. Additional copies are sometimes used to send to accounting for the encumbrance of funds and to the Library of Congress for ordering printed catalog cards. Many libraries also file a copy of the order in the card catalog to alert patrons that a title is on order.

Books ordered direct from publishers often arrive within two to four weeks. Wholesalers also make first shipments within this time, but back orders to publishers for titles not in stock may cause subsequent deliveries to take up to three months. Books ordered from foreign countries often take more than three months. The claiming schedule set by a library must reflect these conditions.

Claiming

Claiming is one of the activities that libraries often forego because of the pressure of other work. When claiming, each order must be scrutinized to determine whether the imprint date warrants the preparation of a claim. A current year's imprint may not yet be published. Second-hand items ordered from dealer catalogs normally should not be claimed—especially if other items ordered from the same source have arrived—since they have probably been sold. Orders sent to foreign vendors should be claimed several weeks later than domestic orders. When the claim is made, the vendor should be given as much information as possible about the original order.

Most cancellations of orders occur at the end of a time specified in the original order, usually 90 days for domestic orders. It is normally not necessary to send a cancellation notice to the vendor when a cancellation clause has been included in the original order. Cancellations for other reasons often require an explanation since they may reach the vendor after the processing of the order has begun.

Receiving the Material

Upon the arrival of the material in the library, the shipment must be unpacked, sorted, matched to the correct order(s) and checked in. The person checking in an item must determine not only that the author, title and edition are what were ordered, but that the item is checked in against its appropriate order, rather than another order for the same title. Control of incoming shipments can be a particular problem in a large library. Not all packages will be properly identified. Inadequately labeled packages can be a particular problem when the item enclosed is part of a series which the library may have on standing order. The item may, therefore, be checked in on the wrong order record. Matching materials with orders filed by main entry can be especially difficult when there is no clear personal author on the item. Often the information on the original form does not correctly describe the item. The price and discount or service charge must also be checked against the encumbrance or the purchase agreement maintained with the vendor.

After the item arrives, the parts of the multiple-copy form are used in a variety of ways. One may be stamped with the date received and filed in an in-process file; another may be sent to accounting to indicate receipt and authorizing payment to be made; yet another will probably accompany the item to cataloging. After the item has been cataloged and the catalog cards filed—if the library uses a card catalog—a copy of the form can be returned to acquisitions to indicate that the item's record can be pulled from the in-process file. A copy of the form may be sent to the person who requested the item indicating that it has been received and cataloged.

Vouching for Payment

When a vendor's invoice is received it must be checked to ensure that the item was received and the amount billed corresponds with the amount encumbered. When the invoice is approved, it is normally sent to a separate office—often outside the library—for payment. The library must maintain a record of the payments it has approved and must correct the encumbrances and balances on its accounts.

While many libraries maintain rather simple accounting records consisting only of the amount currently encumbered or set aside for outstanding orders, the encumbrances cancelled or paid, and the unencumbered balance, an increasing number of libraries allocate their funds by library service units or subject areas to assure a balanced expenditure of funds. A library may establish only a few allocations, such as for renewal of subscriptions, to pay for standing orders and for the replacement of worn and missing items. The balance of the funds might be retained in a general fund from which all other purchases are made.

Public libraries often divide funds by departments such as reference, audiovisual or business, as well as by branches. Separate allocations are usually made for adult and juvenile materials. Many academic libraries make allocations for the use of departments, schools and colleges while retaining funds for standing orders, serials, replacements, reference materials and very expensive items. In recent years it has become common to retain collection development specialists or bibliographers on the library staff, each of whom is provided with an allocation. Some libraries control the rate of encumbering through the periodic release. This is commonly done quarterly so that all funds are not committed too early in the year.

The typical academic library may also have dozens of accounts created by gifts from alumni and friends. It is not uncommon for a single week's orders to contain titles which are charged to the general acquisitions fund and several dozen gift funds, with each item also charged to an allocation. In a manual environment, this may require sorting the orders by account, allocation, and again by the main entry or title for filing into the outstanding order file.

ACQUISITIONS OPERATIONS IN LARGER LIBRARIES

Acquisitions operations change as the size of a library increases. The smallest libraries often record their orders in a loose-leaf binder or in a small card file. Many special libraries order most of their titles by telephone and prepare and mail no purchase orders at all.

When a library is ordering hundreds of items a year and sending out orders on a weekly basis, lists in loose-leafs become cumbersome and do not provide sufficient access points to outstanding orders. The library may then begin to use multiple-copy order forms.

If a library has hundreds of orders outstanding at one time, maintaining records of several items on a single purchase order becomes tedious. Therefore, it is common to assign a separate order number to each item ordered. Many of these separate orders may be combined and mailed to the vendor in one envelope.

The vendor may ship and bill many items together as long as each is identified by its order number. A problem with the use of three-inch by five-inch order forms is that most accounting offices are poorly equipped to maintain order files in this format. Rather than transcribe all orders onto standard 8½-inch by 11-inch purchase orders, many libraries issue open purchase orders to vendors from which they order regularly and then follow-up throughout the year with sub-orders or authorizations on multiple-copy forms.

The organization of an acquisitions unit also changes as the size of the operation grows. The most common division of a unit consisting of more than ten people is by type of activity or method of acquisition: firm order purchasing (the one-time purchases made by a unit called the order or acquisitions department or division), continuations (the ongoing purchases made by a unit called the serials or periodicals department or division), and exchange and gift. Documents may also be broken out. Serials and documents acquisitions are often combined with the recording or cataloging units for these types of materials.

The acquisition of serials is closely related to their recording, since serial recording confirms the receipt of materials not only for technical services personnel, but also for the public. A serial record is usually separate from the catalog because it is deemed uneconomical to enter the receipt of each issue in a card catalog or Computer-Output Microform (COM) catalog. Instead, only the first issue or volume is cataloged and a cross reference is placed in the catalog directing the user to the serials record. The separation of serials, and to a lesser extent documents, from the general acquisitions process has led to the development of quite different acquisitions procedures. The so-called automated acquisitions systems are almost always designed to control firm orders, while the automated systems which support serials activities are called serials control systems. This book focuses on automated acquisitions systems.

Acquisitions statistics vary a great deal from institution to institution. The common ones are the number of requests received, the number returned as already in the library or on order, the number of items ordered, the number of items received, the number of unintentional duplicates and similar information. Few libraries have more sophisticated statistical information such as details about vendor performance or discount patterns.

In acquisitions, as in circulation, most of the staff is likely to be clerical. Only in larger libraries will there be more than a single professional, usually heading the various components of the acquisitions unit and performing such selection as may be the responsibility of the department. Almost all searching, order preparation, check in and processing of invoices will be done by clerical personnel.

In the past the automation of ordering has been particularly attractive to large libraries because in an automated ordering system there is a marked reduction in the manual searching of files and the amount of paperwork produced.

Today acquisitions automation is of interest to libraries of all sizes and types because there are so many options available, each appealing to different motivations and needs.

IMPORTANT AUTOMATED ACQUISITIONS SYSTEMS FEATURES

The author contacted a number of libraries to determine what features were important in an automated acquisitions system. The following were the most frequently cited:

1) Data base access
2) Name/address file
3) Purchase order writing
4) Online ordering
5) In-process file
6) Claiming
7) Receiving/paying
8) Funds accounting
9) Management information
10) Vendor monitoring

While these do not cover all of the features in a typical system, they represent a good basis for comparing systems.

Although gifts, blanket orders and exchange items enter the processing later than orders originating from within the library or from individual requesters, these acquisitions must be included in subsequent operations. The following discussion assumes that materials acquired in any of these ways are to be handled by the automated system.

The functions of the computer in an ordering system can be thought of on three levels: 1) machine processing of specific routine tasks, such as preparation of orders, posting to fund accounts, preparation of reports; 2) machine monitoring of the flow of materials through the system, based primarily on the maintenance of an "in-process" file; and 3) machine assistance to management in scheduling work loads, pinpointing problem areas and reporting on performance.

Data Base Access

Access to a data base is frequently cited as an essential requirement for an automated acquisitions system, but librarians often mean quite different things when they stipulate this feature. Some want access to their own data base to determine whether an item has already been ordered, and to retrieve bibliographic records when a reorder is intended. Others want access to the data base of a bibliographic utility so that a full bibliographic record can be captured for order preparation and for loading into the local system. Still others want access to the data base of a book jobber to determine availability and prices of materials. Access to all three types of data bases might be considered essential by some.

A library may use an automated acquisitions system for pre-order searching on a title it has decided to order, to retrieve bibliographic information about the title, and display information regarding the status of any copy (or copies) on order, in process, in the collection or in circulation. The operator can search for a bibliographic record by using any one of a number of search keys: author, title, call number, ISBN/ISSN, LCCN, etc.

If the operator cannot find the bibliographic record in the file, a new bibliographic record might be entered; or if the library belongs to a bibliographic utility such as OCLC, the operator can search the utility's data base and strip off the records of interest to create the acquisitions record. No additional keying of bibliographic information is required.

Search tools often do not provide current out-of-print, out-of-stock, not-yet-published or publisher-cancelled reasons for book unavailability. Therefore, libraries experience order cancellation rates of from 10% to 25%. The ability to search the data base of a major wholesaler to obtain such information in advance reduces a library's workload by minimizing cancellations and reducing needless order writing, fund accounting, etc.

Name/Address File

A single library may place orders with more than a thousand publishers in the course of a year. Manual files of vendor names and addresses can be laborious to maintain. An automated system can support a name and address file, with online editing capability to make changes, for all publishers the library uses. This will eliminate repetitive typing of names and addresses on orders and claims.

In the case of a turnkey system, the vendor may provide not only the software for the name and address file, but also a basic file of names and addresses, which the library must then maintain. A bibliographic utility can offer a shared name/address file which any of the participating libraries can update. This feature is deemed quite important by directors of large libraries and by heads of libraries with limited reference collections.

Purchase Order Writing

It is taken for granted that any automated acquisitions system can be used to write purchase orders.

The system, if it is to be considered "user-cordial," should lead the operator through an ordering checklist to ensure that the operator is required to enter the appropriate information. After the bibliographic information has been recorded, either by capturing it from a data base or by key-boarding it using a formatted screen for guidance, the location and quantity data are entered. The operator might also establish the order type (rush or normal), the payment type (prepaid or regular), the vendor and the shipping instructions. After the vendor and order type are entered, a claiming date can be established from information maintained in the system or by the operator.

As orders are entered, encumbrances might be immediately updated. If the order results in the near depletion of a fund, the system should warn the operator.

After all the order information and the date of order have been entered into the system, a purchase order can be generated at will or at the time specified. The operator might specify all purchase orders, a specific purchase order number or the purchase orders for a particular vendor.

While a system might not have the capability to handle serials check in and control, librarians expect it to accommodate the preparation of serials orders, including renewal orders.

Online Ordering

The ability to transmit orders online to the desired vendor has been available in wholesaler provided systems, and is under development by at least one bibliographic utility, OCLC.

With an online ordering system, order transmission should be accomplished at the same session in which pre-order searching and order form preparation take place; a dramatic improvement over current mail delivery times. This could save a library the costs involved with batching and other control procedures for mailing orders. An additional benefit of online ordering is that an order cannot be lost or delayed in the mail—this saves a library from having to reissue lost or unaccounted-for orders.

Online ordering to a single wholesaler has been available for several years, but the design problems associated with multi-wholesaler/publisher ordering are significant. For multi-wholesaler ordering the acquisitions system has to interface with several different types of hardware, software, file structures and command languages. BISAC, a book industry standards committee, has been working on a format for sending messages. In spring 1982 OCLC, WLN, CLSI and DataPhase announced agreement to adopt the BISAC order format, but no actual online order transmissions are expected before late 1983.

Online ordering is particularly important to public libraries that want to get best sellers onto the shelves as soon as their patrons begin asking for them.

In-process File

This file, or combination of files, provides the machine record describing the progress of each order through the system. Each record should include a purchase order number and bibliographic information giving the author's name and title in full, as well as the ISBN/ISSN, LC card number, etc. It should also include information about the vendor, the status of the account to which the item is to be charged and an indication of the present status of the item. It should be possible to access the system by any one of several keys such as author, title, uniform title, etc.

In an online system, the in-process file(s) should be available for direct access in response to any information inquiry, or for amendment or enhancement; features limited only by the capacity of the system to handle the interrogation activity levels. In this way, the status of items on order or being processed is up-to-date and can be accessed immediately without the delays and potential for inaccuracies inherent in print-outs from a batch system. This information is of value not only to staff, but also to patrons who inquire about materials not yet on the shelf.

All files should be maintained online in real time so that immediate inquiries can be made for full information about any title. When an online system is used, a back-up record is required. This can be on tape, microform or even a hard-copy.

In summary, the in-process file gives information on those items that are on order, indicating their current status. Online access to this file is considered a basic feature of any modern automated acquisitions system.

Claiming

Claiming is an area where an automated system can also be helpful. If an order is not received within the specified period, a claims notice can be generated to be sent to the vendor unless some notification of delay is received and noted on the system. A system would normally provide for both automatic claiming of ordered materials and operator initiated claims. The system should arrange the items to be claimed in vendor order and print all claims to a vendor on a single claim notice, unless the library requires them to be printed on separate forms. Statistics on the number of claims by vendor should be maintained for a vendor performance report.

Orders may be cancelled automatically if the number of days after claim notices exceeds the library-specified number. The operator might also initiate cancellation of outstanding orders. All financial updating required as a result of cancellation would automatically be handled by the system.

Each vendor record should contain information that tells the system when it should automatically produce a claim letter for a particular purchase order. It should be possible to override this feature when a vendor reports that a title is temporarily out of stock or that there has been a delay in the publishing of a volume.

Receiving/Paying

When an order is received, the material is checked in on the system. In an automated system, when material is checked in the accounts should be automatically adjusted so that funds are moved from encumbrance status to paid-out status. The invoice number and the amount should be kept together in the system until a check is written for the appropriate vendor. If the price of an item has changed since the time of order, the price field in the order record should be updated. The funds would then be automatically adjusted.

The receipt function should provide for all processing associated with checking invoices, receiving shipments, returning materials, routing items, authorizing payment of invoices and keeping the vendor and fund accounting up to date.

When titles are received, a user should be able to retrieve the appropriate acquisitions record to verify the correctness and completeness of the order. A variety of receiving statuses, plus a free-text facility, should allow a user to indicate the precise disposition of the items received. For titles received without purchase orders (approval plans, etc.), an acquisitions record should be created at this stage so that the order can be tracked through the later stages of acquisitions (fund expenditures, invoicing, reports, etc.).

These capabilities are particularly important to libraries which order materials in a variety of ways: firm orders, standing orders, blanket orders, etc.

Funds Accounting

The computer can be particularly valuable in funds accounting. The appropriate fund should be encumbered as soon as the material is ordered. Reports on the status of all the funds should be produced periodically, showing the encumbered and expended totals for each fund and providing up-to-the-minute information on the free balances available on funds. Such a system was operational as early as 1966 at the Brown University Library. It is reported to have reduced clerical time by about 20 hours per month and also to have given tighter control of funds accounting.

When a request for material is received, the cost should be assigned to the fund stipulated by the requester or authorized for that particular type of purchase. An order may be assigned to one or many fund accounts, allowing shared costing. This facility should allow very complex orders to be defined and should handle many types of orders such as rush, continuations, standing orders, confirming orders, gifts, no cost orders, prepaid orders, multivolume/multi-copy orders, etc.

Closely related to funds accounting is check writing or the preparation of vouchers. All files should immediately reflect that a check has been written and that encumbrances and paid-out balances have changed.

This feature is important to virtually all sizes and types of libraries.

Management Information

Management information should include not only summary reports on expenditures, funds balances and related financial information, but also vendor performance reports and statistical reports on the number of items and titles acquired for each library unit over a specified period of time. When the acquisitions system is interfaced with circulation, collection use statistics should also be summarized to facilitate selection.

A recently completed study at the University of Pittsburgh Library has evoked considerable discussion and controversy about acquisition policies in libraries. The study determined that the acquisition practices followed by the University of Pittsburgh Library resulted in only 56% of the newly acquired material actually circulating. Heaviest use occurred in the two-year period following acquisition; a book had only a small probability of circulating if it had not done so within five years of acquisition.

This suggests that much more analysis of circulation use data should be undertaken in planning collection development. Library administrators are becoming more concerned about having reliable and usable management information. The size of a library is less important than a concern about effective management.

Vendor Monitoring

The vendor file should be created and maintained online, possibly as part of the in-process file. A formatted screen should prompt a user for required vendor information. A vendor file may be printed out for a hard-copy listing of all vendors used by the library. The vendor file should be accessible by either vendor name or number.

In addition to vendor name and address, the vendor file should include a claim cycle, established by the library, to indicate how long the system should wait after ordering to produce claims to that vendor. It also should include vendor performance statistics, maintained and calculated by the system, that show the average time taken by a particular vendor to fill an order. Discount information should be retained in the file. A vendor statement showing debits and credits posted to a vendor's account should also be available. The vendor file would normally be linked to the check production feature.

This feature is particularly important to libraries that use many vendors and that cannot, therefore, rely on staff memories to evaluate vendor requirements and performance.

3

Integration or Linkage

An integrated system is one in which several functions share a common data base, and all functions can be accessed using a common sign-on and related commands. The alternative to handling several functions on a single system is to perform them on two or more separate systems and link the systems electronically, so that a user can move from one function to another on a single terminal even though accessing different computers.

At the present time libraries use the data base of a bibliographic utility to achieve low-cost cataloging. It is, therefore, necessary either to adopt the integrated system offered by the utility or to have a link ("interface") between the bibliographic utility's computer system and the system on which the automated acquisitions software is maintained. Most libraries that have chosen not to use integrated systems rely on a bibliographic utility for cataloging and a turnkey system for acquisitions. Therefore, most of the existing links are between bibliographic utilities and turnkey systems.

A library may decide that while it likes a turnkey vendor's system for circulation and an online catalog, it would prefer to use a book jobber's acquisitions system because it includes an online ordering capability. Ideally, there would be an interface between the in-house turnkey system and that of the jobber. The ability to communicate with the systems of other nearby libraries with which the library engages in cooperative collection development would again involve interfaces. A library might be seeking to link four or more systems were it to exercise all of these options.

CONNECTING CPUs WITHIN A SYSTEM

Many of the computers installed in libraries are too small to support multiple functions. Therefore, it may be necessary to replace the central processing unit (CPU) with a larger one or to add a second CPU which is linked to the first to increase the system's processing capacity.

Links between systems with identical hardware and software have only recently been established in the library environment. Local interfacing by wiring two or more CPUs together in one building is well within the state of the art, although as of late 1981 only one multi-CPU system had been installed in a library—a CLSI prototype at the Baltimore County Public Library. CLSI was pressed to develop such a linkage because the CPUs it has available to it are limited in their capacities.

Other turnkey system vendors have, for the most part, sought to transport their software to larger computers to avoid the linking of computers. The initial programming language chosen and dramatic increases in the sizes of computers have made this approach possible for Cincinnati Electronics and DataPhase. Only Geac Ltd. has regularly wired two computers together—for banking applications.

In early 1982 DataPhase was installing a multiple-CPU system for the Chicago Public Library using Tandem computers, which are particularly well suited for this purpose. Tandem uses a device called a Dynabus to move data among computers in a single location. Through special wiring, data are moved at a rate of 26 million characters a second, more than six times the rate at which data normally move between separate CPUs in a computer system. OCLC uses this approach to wire together a number of Tandem computers for communications and disk control. There are 50 Tandems at OCLC and as many as 14 are directly tied together.

Telecommunications and special networking software, rather than direct wiring, are required to link identical systems which are at some distance from one another. This is also feasible given the present level of technology.

LINKING "FOREIGN" SYSTEMS

Today, a library or group of libraries that automates must not only deal with the question of linking the CPUs in a single system or interfacing two identical systems at some distance from each other, but also with the possible need to link its system with a "foreign" system. There are two ways of linking such systems: computer-to-computer and terminal-to-computer.

While computer-to-computer links are particularly difficult to achieve, direct communication between different systems enables full access to, and control of, all files, except as limited by administrative considerations. Using such an interface a library can update the records on any of the linked computers, as well as search them.

The more limited terminal-to-computer approach has been successfully implemented between the terminals of all major turnkey systems and the major bibliographic utility, OCLC. By 1982 the development of interfaces between the vendors and other bibliographic utilities was just beginning.

The Constraints

The movement of bibliographic data among dissimilar systems faces technical, economic and political obstacles that require some analysis. Most of the initial research and application in the area of computer-to-computer linkages appears to have been motivated by the desire to fully use expensive computer resources rather than to facilitate the movement of large amounts of information. Most of the oldest computer networks link large mainframe computers in several large computing centers. More recent work has focused on distributed processing, the creation of multi-processor systems for large companies and government agencies that wish to decentralize their computer systems while retaining central control.

In distributed processing, a large number of minicomputers have typically been dispersed geographically and all have been linked with a host computer at a central site. With few exceptions, these distributed systems have had a highly centralized structure, with most of the processing power concentrated in one large central installation. This has been the case because highly centralized systems have been easier to design, operate and control than decentralized systems. Even though distributed systems might involve more than one type of hardware, to date they have been centrally planned so that software can be developed for the total system, thus avoiding multi-jurisdictional problems.

In the library environment we are seeking to link systems that have been fully and independently developed. Such an effort involves connecting computer systems with different hardware and different software, using various programming languages, some of which are proprietary and confidential. There may also be different file structures, operational features, command languages, record access methods, indexing methods, system performance priorities, and so forth.

Most important, the competing vendors may have little incentive to cooperate with one another. The vendor that is the most firmly established benefits from the inability of other systems to interconnect with its system. If a library planning to purchase a system places a high priority on linkages with one or more existing systems, the lack of appropriate interfaces may force it to select the system(s) that are already installed rather than to select the system that best meets its unique needs.

Computer-to-Computer Communication

Successful computer-to-computer communication among "foreign" or dissimilar systems requires the adoption of protocols or standards for linking systems. At present there are no protocols for the electronic communication of digital information among library systems in a network. A number of protocols have been developed for other applications. These might be used in the development of protocols for libraries, but a great deal of additional work would have to be done.

There is a proposed protocol for libraries which was developed by a task force appointed by the National Commission on Libraries and Information Science (NCLIS) and the National Bureau of Standards (NBS). However, it has not progressed much since the task force made its recommendations in 1977.

The NCLIS/NBS task force protocol would allow different computer systems to inter-act when performing tasks at comparable application levels, regardless of differences in computer architecture or operating systems. The formulation of this protocol represents the completion of one major, time-consuming technical task in laying the groundwork for a multi-system library network, but much remains to be done. The work done by the task force encompassed only the linking of bibliographic utilities, the Library of Congress and other major nodes in a national cataloging and reference service network. The task force specifically recommended that acquisitions and circulation control be handled locally by turnkey systems, and made no provision for linking these systems with one another or with any emerging national network.

The Canadian Computerized Bibliographic Centre Study by the National Library of Canada, a much more detailed study of library networks than any undertaken in the United States, concludes:

"... [It] might be quite unrealistic to attempt a high level of standardization in a field that includes a growing number of private sector organizations and has generally favoured a laissez-faire approach. Also, a number of incompatibilities . . . cannot easily be standardized. . . . The [National Library of Canada should] concentrate its efforts on the development of computer-to-computer links between shared-cataloguing systems . . . and NCL should promote the development of protocols for such highspeed links."[1]

Thus, the two national efforts to develop protocols for libraries are of little help to libraries attempting to connect local systems with one another or with the systems of distant suppliers. Too little work has been done, and the thrust of the recommendations is to focus national efforts on the linking of shared-cataloging systems.

The author interviewed several turnkey system vendors in 1981. While none refused to consider the development of a computer-to-computer interface with systems supplied by other vendors, all qualified their responses. One firm insisted that the cost would be pro-hibitive because it would take in excess of 100 man-years to develop the software. Three other estimates fell in the range of four to 20 man-years. One vendor stated that he could not sign a contract to participate in such development unless a vendor performance measurement tool were developed, so he could be paid when he had performed his share of the specified work. This arrangement would protect the vendor against the possibility of nonpayment because of another vendor's failure or unwillingness to perform. A library or library consortium that agreed to this approach might incur substantial expense without achieving a working interface.

In short, while computer-to-computer linkage between "foreign" systems is technically feasible, it will probably be several years before the obstacles are overcome. The creation of standards is essential to the development of this capability.

Terminal-to-Computer Interfaces

At the beginning of 1982 the only successful linkage between "foreign" library systems was through terminal-to-computer interfacing. This involves using the terminal of one automated system to access the computer of another automated system. For example, DataPhase customers in Maryland are successfully searching CLSI and Systems Control systems throughout the state. The one-time cost of each such interface can range from practically nothing to $90,000 in software development. Several other vendors have expressed a willingness to develop the necessary interfaces, although some said such development would have a lower priority than developing linkages for their own systems. CLSI, for example, is most concerned with linking CPUs that are standing next to one another. Cincinnati Electronics is attempting to develop statewide linkages of its own systems.

Several library administrators and staff interviewed by the author said they would prefer to limit linkage to the searching and message capability provided by the terminal-to-computer interfaces rather than to provide computer-to-computer interfacing which would permit libraries and vendors to manipulate one another's systems and files. Since the terminal-to-computer link would meet the expressed requirements it would not be necessary to fund expensive computer-to-computer development. The development of the computer-to-computer interface is contingent on libraries specifying this capability when procuring a system.

THE NORTH SUBURBAN EXPERIENCE

The North Suburban Library System (NSLS) in Illinois has encountered serious operational problems with its system. The NSLS linked seven separate installations of the system used by the 22 libraries in the consortium. The NSLS system specifications required that the vendor (CLSI) provide a computer-to-computer interface, but as this has not yet been accomplished, terminal-to-terminal interfaces are being used. This means that an operator must dial up one system at a time, log on and conduct a search, repeating the process for each system until the required item is located. In addition, the idiosyncracies in the locally developed data bases mounted on each system require that the operator be familiar with each separate one.

FRONT-END PROCESSORS AS EMULATORS

The libraries of the greater Denver-Boulder, CO, area—known as the Irving Group—have recently received a report from Arthur Young Consultants on the general design and implementation of a data communications network connecting the computer systems in the five libraries. The libraries in the group use either CLSI or DataPhase automated library systems. The consultants have recommended the use of front-end processors functioning as interfaces between each individual CPU and the telephone line. The interface will be programmed to emulate a computer terminal, which will be recognized by both the CLSI and DataPhase systems as if it were one of the system's "own" internal library terminals. Thus, neither turnkey vendor will need to modify its system. The transmission medium among libraries will be conventional voice-grade telephone lines. Other libraries may be able to participate in the network by dial-up. Over five years the cost of the venture will be in excess of $450,000 because hardware must be purchased, programs written and telecommunications costs paid.

In late 1981 the Irving Group solicited proposals from firms qualified to undertake the detailed system design. In early 1982, it was raising funds for the project. If the venture is successful, an interface may become available that will make it possible for a terminal operator to sequentially dial up several other systems without being expert in the unique protocols and characteristics of each. It is hoped that the cost of this capability will drop dramatically after the initial installation in Colorado. Once the concept of interfacing by emulation among the systems of major turnkey vendors is well established, other interfaces are likely to be developed.

4
Costs, Ease of Adoption and Vendor Reliability

One of the major issues in considering automation is the cost of implementing and operating an automated system. Two cost factors that must be examined are the ease of adopting and discontinuing a system and the reliability of the vendor. Reliance on a vendor that quotes its service on a monthly subscription basis may be more expensive than acquiring the hardware and software from a turnkey vendor. However, if the turnkey system is not yet fully developed it may be better to select the more expensive month-by-month option, which can be discontinued without the loss of substantial capital funds. A very low price from a vendor that has not established its financial viability may be shortsighted. In this chapter each of these considerations will be discussed.

COSTS IN AUTOMATING ACQUISITIONS

The price quoted by a vendor may be misleading. The comparison of either the start-up costs only or the operating costs only for each of several options will give a distorted picture of the actual impact of a system on a library's budget over a period of time. For example, a bibliographic utility system involves a very low initial outlay, but for a major library the operating costs can be substantial, possibly resulting in a higher outlay over five years than might be required were a turnkey system to be purchased. Even the seemingly high initial price quoted for a turnkey system is usually only half the true cost of such a system over a period of five years. The five-year cost of a turnkey system is normally at least triple the purchase price if a library chooses to lease the system rather than purchase it outright.

Not all costs will be incurred with each automation option. It is, therefore, necessary to make a checklist of cost elements and enter the figures for each option. By adding up all of the costs that might be incurred over a five-year period, the true cost of the options can be determined. The checklist should include:

   a.   Data processing personnel

b. Central site processing equipment
c. Data storage
d. Terminals
e. Telecommunications hardware
f. Software
g. Installation and training
h. Site preparation
i. Conversion of records
j. Telecommunications
k. Maintenance
l. Supplies
m. Use fees

Acquisitions personnel costs are not included as a separate element in the above list because nonrecurring personnel costs are normally incorporated into several of the elements on the list and ongoing personnel costs tend to be similar regardless of which automated system is used. The comparison of staffing requirements for the manual system versus the most attractive automated system will, of course, have to be made if the library's motivation for considering automation is cost reduction or containment.

None of the options except in-house development involve the hiring of data processing personnel. Virtually none of the 300 or more turnkey systems which have been installed are staffed with full-time data processing personnel. The normal practice is to have the regular library staff oversee the system. While no special background is required, training is necessary for both the system supervisor and terminal operators. The person designated as supervisor must be able to work well with the vendor's technical personnel. Bibliographic utility and jobber systems require even less supervision than a turnkey system.

Elements b through i on the checklist are one-time costs; the rest are recurring costs. Each vendor's approach to pricing will result in different costs for several of these elements. What is gained in one element may be lost in another. In order to make a valid comparison, it is necessary to consider the system costs over a period of several years. Typically, five years is the period during which a system can be expected to function without major overhaul. It is also the amortization period commonly used by accountants when depreciating this type of equipment.

In-house Systems

In-house systems normally involve the highest one-time costs because hardware must be purchased (elements b, c, d and e) and a site will have to be prepared (element h). The cost of software development will normally be from 50% to 80% of the total cost of the system. A typical medium-sized system might involve the investment of $200,000 in hardware and from $200,000 to $800,000 in software development costs (primarily cost element a). The software costs can be reduced by transferring an existing software package. The most attractive packages cost from $50,000 to $100,000 each and require at least another $100,000 to adapt. An in-house acquisitions system might, therefore, cost a minimum of $350,000 in initial hardware and software expenses.

It would be possible, of course, to have the acquisitions system share a computer with other functions, library or non-library. In that case some of the expenses could be charged against the other functions. This is true for both in-house and turnkey systems. When a system performs several diffeent functions the costs are normally allocated among them on the basis of the number of transactions performed. A library performing both circulation and acquisitions functions on a turnkey system might charge less than 5% of the system's cost to the acquisitions function. Normally, when a library adds acquisitions to an installed turnkey system, only the incremental or add-on cost is charged to the acquisitions function. This would consist mainly of the cost of the acquisitions software and the cost of additional terminal(s) and printer(s).

Turnkey Systems

The typical turnkey system also involves a considerable initial expenditure for hardware and software. Table 4.1 illustrates the cost breakdown of a medium-sized turnkey system.

The minimum cost for a minicomputer-based turnkey system would be at least $125,000. A micro-based system with the same features, but with slower processing speed and capability, might cost as little as $75,000. The additional cost of a system larger than that illustrated in Table 4.1 would normally be reflected in the first three lines, while the last two would remain approximately the same. Vendor pricing and bidding practices vary a great deal depending on policies, competitive position, levels of inventory, commitment of personnel, etc. Software pricing can be difficult to calculate. For example, a DataPhase quote always includes all future modules, while quotes from other vendors usually do not —unless the vendor is seeking to be highly competitive. If the software isn't "bundled" (i.e., packaged) in a single price, each module can cost from $20,000 to $50,000.

Telecommunications hardware can cost from $500 to $4000 per terminal, depending on whether a simple modem is used or more expensive multiplexing hardware is installed to make it possible for terminals to share leased or dedicated lines. (Modems are more common.)

There are a number of other costs which must be added to the above in the case of both in-house developed and turnkey systems. Among them are site preparation, hardware and software maintenance, telecommunications, supplies, conversion of machine-readable files and retrospective conversion of manual files.

Table 4.1 Typical Breakdown of Payment to Vendor
($260,000 System)

Central site hardware	$110,000
Terminals	70,000
Communications hardware	15,000
Software	55,000
Installation and training	10,000

Site Preparation

Site preparation for an in-house or turnkey system configured around a minicomputer normally costs $5000 to $8000, but can exceed $10,000 in older buildings that require additional electrical power and air conditioning. Each of the major turnkey vendors has a site preparation manual setting forth what needs to be done. It is useful to obtain such a manual even if preparing for an in-house system. Full-sized computers require more costly installations than minis. This is a cost which is normally not incurred with the installation of a bibliographic utility or wholesaler system.

Hardware and Software Maintenance

Annual hardware maintenance normally costs up to 5% of the initial purchase price of a piece of equipment. For an in-house system, annual software maintenance should be calculated at 25% of the initial development price. For a turnkey system, a maintenance charge of $400 to $1000 per month normally includes all enhancements or improvements in the software. Maintenance fees are usually incorporated into the system use fees for bibliographic utility and wholesaler systems.

Telecommunications Costs

Telecommunications charges, when projected over five years and incorporating probable rate increases, normally average $7 per mile per month for a leased or dedicated line.)* Bibliographic utilities and wholesalers realize considerably lower rates than a single library can obtain by purchasing telecommunications at bulk rates, or by using value-added networks such as Tymnet or Telenet. However, telecommunications costs—a major factor in bibliographic utility and wholesaler systems—are not normally encountered with in-house or turnkey systems: only terminals outside the building housing the central site require telephone lines; terminals inside the building are wired directly to the central site. Libraries that share an automated system with other libraries will incur telecommunications costs. If there are enough terminals involved, telecommunications costs can be reduced by using multiplexors or other devices which permit multiple terminals to share a single leased telephone line. This hardware may increase the capital cost by as much as $4000 per terminal.

Conversion Charges

A library which has previously kept acquisitions records in machine-readable form can have a service bureau convert the records into the format of the new in-house or turnkey system. Converting existing machine-readable files to the operating format of a vendor's system should not cost more than $.01 per record if the library has OCLC or other MARC records. Reformatting records that are not in MARC format normally costs at least $.08 per record and can cost up to $.25 per record. Reformatted records can then be tape loaded into the new system. Some bibliographic utilities and wholesalers do not allow tape loading, but require that all data be entered online.

---

*Projected telecommunications costs are based on estimates by AT&T that rate increases should not average more than 10% compounded over the next five years.

Retrospective conversion of manual records to machine-readable form can cost from approximately $.75 to more than $1.50 per record. This figure includes the cost of labor, whether that of the library or a commercial firm. A library may wish to limit the conversion of existing records to those for standing orders and serials, since existing monographs records should be cleared from the old system upon receipt of the materials or the cancellation of undelivered orders.

Supply costs, primarily for forms, are usually quite comparable for the various automation options. They normally do not exceed $.30 per order produced.

Cost Comparisons

The major costs incurred in bibliographic utility and wholesaler systems are system use fees. Bibliographic utilities charge by the transaction, while wholesalers charge by the month. The rates for bibliographic utilities in late 1981 ranged from $1.50 to $2.50 per order—a figure which has been adjusted to reflect the extra charges for claims and reports. The wholesaler systems normally cost $1100 to $1300 per month.

The total cost of a system over five years will vary quite significantly from option to option. A library processing 10,000 orders a year would spend at least $75,000 to use a bibliographic utility system; $4500 for a terminal and a modem; $12,000 for telecommunications; and $15,000 for supplies. Libraries not relying on the utility's printer would have to spend $5000 more. A wholesaler system would cost $66,000 in fees plus $12,000 for telecommunications and $15,000 in supplies. A turnkey system might involve only the purchase of a terminal and modem at $2500, a printer at $5000, and supplies at $15,000. This is provided the library had already installed adequate central site hardware and had obtained a "bundled" software quotation which reduced the additional software cost to $10,000. The total minimum five-year cost might then be $106,500-$111,500 for a bibliographic utility system, $93,000 for a wholesaler system, and $22,500-$32,500 for a turnkey system.

In contrast a library processing 1000 titles a year would spend $7500 for utility system use fees, $4500 for a terminal and a printer, $12,000 for telecommunications and $1500 for supplies. For a wholesaler system the use cost would remain $66,000 and telecommunications $12,000. Only the supply costs would drop to $1500. For the turnkey system all costs would be the same as for the 10,000 title-per-year library except supply costs which would drop to $1500.

Total minimum cost of the options for a small library could range from $79,500 for the wholesaler system, to $25,500 for a utility system and $19,000 for a turnkey system.

These are minimum costs. The costs for any option, especially the turnkey option, could go much higher. What is clear is that the volume of ordering may have a significant effect on the comparative five-year costs of the options. Table 4.2 illustrates the costs that should be examined for each of the major automated acquisitions options.

Table 4.2 Cost Elements in Automating Acquisitions

	In-house	Turnkey	Utility	Jobber
Data processing personnel	A	N	N	N
Central site processing equipment	A	A	N	N
Data storage	A	A	N	N
Terminals	A	A	A	A
Telecommunications hardware	C	C	A	A
Software purchase	C	A	N	N
Installation and training	A	C	C	C
Site preparation	A	A	N	N
Conversion of records	C	C	C	C
Telecommunications	C	C	A	A
Maintenance	A	A	N	N
Supplies	A	A	A	A
Use Fees	N	N	A	A

Key: A-Always; C-Circumstances vary; N-Never

EASE OF ADOPTION

The relative immaturity of the automated acquisitions systems market and the state of interfacing makes it imperative that libraries consider the ease of adoption and discontinuation of the system that initially appears most attractive. The expenditure of several thousand dollars for hardware and software usually commits a library for five or more years. If the system is incomplete or lacks many of the features the library wants, a long-term commitment of this type should be avoided. The library may postpone the automation of acquisitions or it might adopt an interim system. The systems offered by wholesalers are available on a month-to-month basis. The cost is relatively high for all but large libraries ordering 10,000 or more titles a year. Nevertheless, even a charge of $1000 per month may be justified for a library processing 3000 titles a year if it has pressing needs and all of the other options require a major capital outlay.

A bibliographic utility system is normally less expensive on a monthly basis for most libraries because no monthly minimum charge is levied. A library can even opt to perform its acquisitions work on the terminal(s) it acquires for cataloging. It will then incur only the transaction charge of $2 (or slightly more) per item ordered.

Conversely, a library that obtained its acquisitions software as part of a single or "bundled" software price at the time it installed a turnkey circulation control or a patron access catalog can try out the vendor's acquisitions subsystem with minimum outlay or risk.

One must look at more than direct costs, however. The introduction of an automated acquisitions system will change the duties of staff members and may affect the organization of the library's administrative units. A second change, a few months after introducing an automated system, could be disruptive and demoralizing. Any interim system should be easy to learn and similar to the subsequent system the library might procure. The interim system should be installed for no less than six months and the transfer period from one system to another should be planned to take at least three months.

Adopting an interim system should be considered an exceptional course of action rather than the normal approach to automation. In the case of acquisitions automation it is a more likely course of action than in the case of circulation control, because none of the automated acquisitions options available are mature products. For circulation control, virtually all of the available systems are offered by well-established turnkey vendors and have been available for several years. It is, therefore, easier to select a circulation control system.

VENDOR RELIABILITY

The reliability of a vendor selected to supply automated acquisitions support should be evaluated both in terms of past record of responsiveness to clients and financial strength. A library can expect many small problems and some major ones to arise when it is installing and using software that is still under development. A library can determine how well a vendor responds to customer concerns by calling several of the vendor's customers at random, particularly customers that are similar to it in size and type. Even if the vendor has no established record in acquisitions automation, one can still learn a great deal about the vendor's responsiveness in providing circulation, cataloging, book wholesaling or other services.

Financial strength is important because there are more vendors in the automated acquisitions system market than can be supported by the potential number of sales. If a vendor is offering acquisitions automation as part of a series of related automation products or services, and the older products or services are profitable, there is a good chance that the vendor will continue to offer acquisitions automation support for several years. If a vendor offers only acquisitions automation it is considerably more vulnerable to an extremely competitive market environment.

The wholesalers present a particularly interesting case. They offer only acquisitions automation, but they do not look at the service solely from the standpoint of its direct profit potential. Additional benefits accrue because the online ordering component of a wholesaler's acquisitions system can reduce order fulfillment costs and can make customers less willing to undertake a change in vendor. Nevertheless, a wholesaler may abandon its systems if it determines that interfaces between its in-house computer systems and the online ordering subsystems of bibliographic utility or turnkey vendors will have the same desired effect on order fulfillment costs; that the pattern of changing vendors is not affected by the availability of a proprietary acquisitions system; and that a proprietary system does not contribute to profits.

Should a bibliographic utility realize too low a level of acquisitions services to have the established fees pay for the human and data processing resources used, it will probably raise its rates. It is unlikely that it will discontinue the service because, as a not-for-profit membership organization, it will be pressed by the participants to continue all services.

A turnkey vendor of multi-function systems may slow ongoing development of an acquisitions module if the function is not widely used by customers and if the availability of the function is not a major factor in new system sales. It therefore is important to determine what number of a turnkey vendor's customers have opted to use the acquisitions module.

The most vulnerable organizations in the acquisitions field are the vendors who offer primarily acquisitions, or who offer it without a substantial base of installed systems of other types. Each installed customer normally represents an income of up to $12,000 a year in software maintenance and enhancement payments. The vendor that has only eight installations will barely take in enough to support a minimum development staff, while the vendor with 40 installations will be able to support sufficient personnel to undertake simultaneous development in several areas.

Determining vendor reliability is critical when undertaking an automated acquisitions system. The library should investigate this carefully and should also be sure that it can shift its dependence to another vendor when necessary with a minimum of cost and disruption.

5
The Ideal System

The ideal acquisitions system would allow an operator to search the library's own bibliographic data base online from any terminal in the library, or even from a remote external location, using any one of several access points such as author, title, keywords of the title, publisher, date of publication, etc. The operator would be able to determine the status—for example, on order, received—of any item by consulting the library's data base.

The system would allow an authorized operator to order additional copies of a title for which an order was previously placed. Not everyone with access to a terminal should be able to perform this and a number of other functions. Thus, passwords or some other form of security would be required to prevent unauthorized actions.

The system would contain a vendor (publisher/wholesaler) address file. There would be online access to a vendor data base which the operator might search, in a predetermined order of preference, to determine which vendors were able to ship the wanted material immediately, and at what price.

The system would be linked to the data base of a bibliographic utility so that bibliographic records would be stripped off to create purchase orders.

The system would be able to access vendors' inventory files which would include status notes for all titles—e.g., the item is out of print, not yet published, scheduled for later publication or scheduled for reprinting. The authorized operator, after determining the appropriate vendor on the basis of availability and/or price, would be able to place the order online to the vendor, preferably directly into the vendor's internal order fulfillment system.

The ideal system would alert the operator if an order about to be transmitted was going to deplete the funds in the account selected. At the time of ordering, the library's financial files would be simultaneously updated to reflect an accurate encumbrance against the appropriate account.

When the order is received by the vendor, the material should be pulled from the inventory and mailed within 24 hours. The jobber's inventory record would be reduced immediately so that the next library inquiring about the title would be given correct inventory status information.

The library using an online acquisitions system would have the flexibility to provide very detailed financial information in a variety of ways. All of the areas and sub-areas against which materials are charged would be accommodated. The ideal system would also be capable of selecting titles from the master data base from which it would produce selection lists in multiple copies. These could be used for selection purposes in large branch systems.

The ideal acquisitions system would maintain a comprehensive online file giving the library complete information about every item on order but not received, as well as everything in process. Other available information would include the date of shipment by the vendor, the date of receipt by the library, the date paid, etc. The system would alert the library when expected materials did not arrive after a predetermined amount of time, so that cancellation or reordering could be undertaken.

The vendor would supply machine-readable invoices with the material. The acquisitions system would verify when all items on the invoice had been received and then write the necessary checks, pre-addressed and ready for mailing. If a library was not authorized to issue checks, the system would generate vouchers for payment. Invoices that had not been cleared would be identified by the system for further investigation. Concurrently with payment, all financial records would be updated (encumbrances cancelled, expenditures posted against the correct accounts, etc.). Also, the in-process file would be updated to reflect the date of receipt and the date of payment, including the check number and other pertinent information. The library would have the capability of converting the machine-readable information in the acquisitions system to a record for circulation control and/or to a catalog record. An online interface with the library's other automated systems would be provided, including linkages with the library's circulation and patron access catalog systems.

The system would be able to accommodate a variety of materials, including monographs, serials, continuations, government documents, deposit accounts, approval plans, blanket orders, gift and exchange agreements, and other categories of materials acquired by the library. The system should provide a complete audit trail by title and by fund for a library-specified length of time online, and then print audit trails on microfiche for permanent retention. Management information of various kinds including vendor performance statistics should be available. It would be possible for the library to determine when service performance was deteriorating or discounts were decreasing. Preferably the system would report exceptions to expected patterns that had been recorded in the system, rather than generating large numbers of reports that require time-consuming review.

There was no single system available in early 1982 that incorporated all of these features. Almost all of the features were in the preliminary design of one or more vendors' systems. It appears unlikely that any system would have all of the features before 1985.

The choice of a system, therefore, involves careful examination of the issues, and selection of the option that best meets the library's current and future needs.

CRITERIA FOR SYSTEMS COMPARISONS

The following checklist of features may be used to compare systems.

A. Files Searching
  1. What files are available for searching?
     a. The library's own holdings?
     b. On order/in-process file(s)? Local and/or union?
     c. Bibliographic utility data bases?
     d. Other bibliographic data bases?
     e. Vendor file(s)?
         (1) Availability or stock information?
         (2) Current list price?
     f. Accounting file(s)?
     g. Vendor name/address file(s)?
  2. How flexible is the searching system?
     a. How many access points are available?
     b. Can partial keys be used? (That is, can an operator key in an incomplete name or word and retrieve all possible matches?)

B. Ordering
  1. Can the system produce selection lists if desired?
  2. Can the system handle multiple copy ordering for different locations easily?
  3. Does the system allow the operator to select the vendor?
  4. Is online ordering (instantaneous transmission) directly to vendor possible?
  5. Can the system print purchase order forms ready for mailing?
  6. Can the system print multiple-part order record sets for internal use if desired?
  7. Are the appropriate funds encumbered at the time of order using an estimated discount for the selected jobber?
  8. Is the operator notified if the funds are exhausted?
  9. Can libraries sharing the systems select different options?

C. Monitoring
  1. Is the in-process file instantaneously updated so that the current status of an order can be determined at any time?
     a. On order
     b. Shipped
     c. Received

2. Is vendor fulfillment status available?
   a. Back ordered
   b. Cancelled
3. Are claim and/or cancellation notices prepared according to the library's specifications?
4. What statistics are provided by the system?
5. What kind of vendor monitoring is available?
6. What exception/error reports are produced?

D.   Receiving/Paying/Accounting
1. Is the in-process file instantaneously updated so that the receipt and/or payment of an item is recorded?
2. Are the various funds updated automatically and correctly (i.e., previous disencumbered and accurate expenditures posted)?
3. Are vendor's invoices balanced and problem invoices identified for manual resolution?
4. Can checks be written automatically after clearing of invoices?
5. Can payment vouchers be issued if the library is not authorized to issue checks?
6. Are audit trails available so that the operator can determine the history of any given order or the history of any given fund?

E.   Interfacing
1. Can the acquisitions system connect with other systems in the library?
   a. Circulation
   b. Serials control
   c. Patron access catalog
2. Can the system interface with the library's bibliographic utility?
3. Can the operator order catalog records at time of order/receipt of material if desired?
4. What machine-readable records can be obtained from or loaded into other systems?

F.   Screen Display
1. What screen displays are provided by the system?
2. Are the screen displays difficult to interpret?
3. Are they compatible with the forms currently used by the staff?
4. Will extensive staff training be required?

G.   Cost Breakdown
1. Does the system vendor itemize costs in enough detail for the library to make realistic comparisons?
2. Are all of the items necessary to make the system operational included in the cost breakdown?
3. Are the costs capital expenses or operational expenses?
4. What commitment is there regarding the costs in future years?

IN-HOUSE SOFTWARE DEVELOPMENT

As the foregoing checklist implies, an ideal system essentially means ideal software. Hardware supplies support only, and there is relatively little difference in equipment available from one vendor to another. Virtually the only way for a library to achieve its ideal system today is to undertake in-house development and design its own online acquisitions software. When doing so, a library maintains a high degree of control over system design, permitting it to specify the inclusion of all desired functions. The cost, however, will be extremely high and unpredictable. As noted in Chapter 4, the cost of software development can represent as much as 80% of the total cost of a computer system. When this cost is carried solely by one library, rather than by many libraries participating in a bibliographic utility, purchasing the same turnkey system or using the same book wholesaler's system, the cost can be several hundred thousand dollars.

Most of the libraries that attempted to develop their own systems did so in the late 1960s and early 1970s. Virtually all of these systems are batch systems for producing purchase orders and controlling funds. Large systems include those at the Universities of British Columbia, California at Berkeley, Columbia, Cornell, Harvard, Syracuse and UCLA. Smaller batch systems were developed at a number of public libraries.

Online acquisitions systems were generally launched in the late 1970s. Among them are the systems of the Howard University Library, University of Minnesota Biomedical Library, Pennsylvania State University Library and Denver University Library. All of the online systems are envisioned as future integrated library systems. Boys Town Center (Boys Town, NE) is developing a small integrated system with automated acquisitions. The Fraser Valley (British Columbia) Regional Library has contracted with a software house to develop its shared automated system.

The library opting for in-house development must decide between a system configured around a full-size computer (probably not located in the library except in the case of a very large library) or around a minicomputer or microcomputer (which probably would be owned by the library). The development of a system designed to be run on an existing full-size computer in the parent organization might appear to be the most reasonable choice until the library begins to explore the cost of software development.

OTHER SOFTWARE OPTIONS

One way of reducing the developmental costs of software is to purchase it from another library or library consortium. The modifications required to meet a specific library's needs will range from minor to extensive and the costs will vary accordingly. The purchase price of the software may range from $2000 to $100,000, but the total software cost may be much higher. A package that requires considerable modification to fit the library's needs and/or is written in a language that is not highly "transportable" to other equipment will add substantially to the purchase cost. This type of approach should only be undertaken by a library that has in-house data processing expertise.

Examples of acquisitions software packages that have been developed for a consortium or a single library and are now available for sale to others include the Washington Library Network's acquisitions subsystem and the Northwestern University Library's NOTIS III (Northwestern On-Line Total Integrated System). The former has recently become available through a vendor as a turnkey system. The latter may be available in the future as an off-the-shelf package with a program for ongoing software enhancements.

Although there are more than 5000 standardized software packages available, virtually none have been developed specifically for libraries. If a library turns to a "software house"—a firm that specializes in the development and sale of software—it can get custom development of software. Custom software packages developed in this way are sometimes later generalized by the firm and become "off-the-shelf" products.

There are hundreds of software houses in North America. Almost every major city has several. The standard practice is for the firm to develop the necessary software for a particular customer on the basis of specifications the library has provided. The price is usually higher than the estimated cost of in-house development by the library, but the price and delivery date are firm if the contract so stipulates. The software house often uses its experience to solicit other clients in the same field. If only minor adaptation of the initial software is required for subsequent clients, the price can be lowered for the buyers and the profitability to the vendor increased. One Texas firm did several circulation system software contracts this way. The first customer can recover some of its high cost by stipulating in its contract that it will receive a royalty on subsequent uses of the software package developed for it.

The maintenance of custom-developed software is also expensive. Again, there is no broad base of libraries over which to spread the cost of making improvements or enhancements. The cost is usually at least $40 per hour for additional programming. Enhancements may affect the original programs so that they too have to be modified.

AVAILABLE SOFTWARE PACKAGES

The balance of this chapter is devoted to summaries of three major software packages: DOBIS/LEUVEN, Maggie's Place and NOTIS. The reason for discussing these software options in a chapter on ideal systems is that the primary justification for choosing a software package is not to cut costs, but to further develop the software in-house to tailor it to the unique needs of the library. In early 1982 there were no ongoing software maintenance/enhancement programs available for either DOBIS/LEUVEN or NOTIS, but there were plans to provide ongoing support for the NOTIS software.

The Washington Library Network software, which is also separately available, is described in Chapter 7 (bibliographic utilities). This is because only three libraries had purchased WLN software as a separate package by early 1982, whereas more than 60 were using it as part of the bibliographic utility service.

DOBIS/LEUVEN

Development of the DOBIS/LEUVEN system (Dortmunder Bibliothekssystem/Leuvens Integraal Bibliotheek System) began in 1971. In that year, the University of Dortmund contracted with IBM of West Germany to develop an integrated online library management system. IBM performed additional work on the system for the University of Leuven, which created an international MARC standard for the system. The combined system supports cataloging, searching, acquisitions and circulation. In general, DOBIS is oriented to technical services and Leuven to public services.

The programs are written in PL/1 and assembler languages, and operate on IBM/370 compatible hardware. The acquisitions module resembles the WLN acquisitions module in that there is no duplication of data in the system. All subsystems share a common bibliographic file. Local information is tied to the shared bibliographic file, but retained separately.

The acquisitions functions that are part of the DOBIS system allow for immediate online additions and updates in all acquisitions files. Records are indexed by vendor, library fund, order and document number as well as by eight bibliographic indexes such as author, title and subject. Added copies can be recorded very quickly. The system also accommodates interlibrary loan activity. Financial and statistical information about vendors and funds can be updated and displayed online. Automatic claiming is performed and can be regulated by the vendor performance statistics maintained online. Order information is created and formatted to the specifications recorded in the vendor profile.

The primary memory requirements depend upon the number of active terminals, the tasks being executed concurrently and the response time desired. The minimum storage required for DOBIS is 512KB (kilobytes).

Since DOBIS/LEUVEN is not just an acquisitions system, or a circulation system, or a cataloging system, but can perform all of these functions, the workload tends to be much higher than the workload placed on a single-function system. The smallest CPU on which DOBIS/LEUVEN will operate is 1MB (megabyte) unless a library opts to perform some functions in batch mode. DOBIS/LEUVEN does not require a dedicated CPU, but can be run concurrently with other, different systems. Therefore, this one megabyte would contain the operating system and the terminal communicating system, and, depending upon usage, it could also be used to perform other functions, such as word processing or computer assisted instruction (CAI).

Minimum system configuration consists of an IBM System/370 Model 138 or comparable machine with appropriate disk storage (based on the size of the data base) and at least one IBM 3270 Display Station, a nine-track tape unit and a high speed printer for printing notices and listings.

The DOBIS/LEUVEN system is not a turnkey system. Rather, it is made up of software packages marketed by IBM to all types of libraries. While DOBIS and LEUVEN may be purchased separately, the acquisitions function may not be purchased separately from the other technical service functions.

IBM will sell the computer with the software, but it will not provide the extensive training and ongoing software enhancements that libraries are accustomed to receiving from turnkey vendors. It is expected that many customers will acquire the software for use on existing equipment, the capacity of which may have to be increased. The system cannot be used without data processing expertise to adapt the purchased software.

As of late 1981 the online DOBIS/LEUVEN software was marketed by IBM at a cost of $1500 per month for 24 months. This price includes the license fee, documentation and source code. Future maintenance and enhancement of the software is not available from IBM.

As with other IBM products, DOBIS/LEUVEN is marketed through IBM marketing representatives located in IBM offices around the country. The availability of the software was announced in the United States in February, 1980. A number of U.S. installations are in progress, but in early 1982 only one was operational—at the Austin (TX) Public Library. The system has also been installed in libraries in Canada, Europe and Africa.

Before IBM was able to obtain the marketing rights to the DOBIS product, the University of Dortmund decided that it would distribute its programs directly to one major library in each interested country. It would be up to each library to modify the product to fit its country's needs. At this point the National Library of Canada (NLC) obtained the DOBIS software directly from the University of Dortmund. The NLC chose to make extensive changes to the software to fit its requirements. To date it has implemented only the cataloging and the catalog search portion of the system from Dortmund. The version of DOBIS installed at Centennial College Bibliocentre (Toronto, Canada) was obtained from NLC. Centennial has made its own modifications to the programs. In addition, before IBM was able to obtain the marketing rights to the LEUVEN product, Centennial purchased a copy directly from the University of Leuven and modified it to correspond to its version of DOBIS. The DOBIS and DOBIS/LEUVEN software in use in Canada are substantially different from the software available from IBM in the United States.

The primary memory required for the NLC version of DOBIS is substantial. Centennial College is nearing saturation on its 2MB machine for its 19-member consortium. This is approximately eight times the primary memory of a typical installed turnkey local cataloging and circulation system. The capacity of the National Library of Canada's mainframe is currently 4MB and is to be upgraded to 6MB–8MB in the future.

Maggie's Place

The Pikes Peak Library District in Colorado Springs, CO, has developed an integrated library system called Maggie's Place. All of Maggie's Place components are designed to operate on a Digital Equipment Corp. (DEC) PDP/11 series computer with the RSTS/E operating system. The price of the hardware, which must be purchased separately from a dealer, ranges from $45,000 to well over $100,000, depending upon the number of terminals and the amount of secondary storage required.

Software for the functions of acquisitions, circulation, community resources, periodicals and administrative tasks are sold by Pikes Peak and can be installed on a DEC PDP for a license fee plus installation and training. Acquisitions software alone costs approximately $8000. There is no ongoing software maintenance or enhancement available at this low price.

Through the acquisitions system, items to be ordered are searched against the library online circulation file, if maintained, as well as the acquisitions file. The acquisitions file contains all items on order, as well as items in process, and includes standing orders that are placed with publishers or which must be renewed annually.

Read-only access can be provided from any terminal in an integrated system and the file can be searched by author, title, vendor or bar code. The system will respond with the information in the data base, including the number of copies on order and in processing.

Through the various functions, staff can search the file by several approaches, load new orders, calculate encumbrances, produce reports arranged by department, area and line item, delete items from the file, generate purchase orders sorted by vendor and title, clear invoices for payment, modify items in the file and record the receipt of items. All materials can be processed through the system except periodicals check-in and claiming. Standing orders are flagged and can be accessed separately. A separate subprogram handles claims.

The system can provide a separate encumbrance report for standing orders and serials by department or division. Orders are now mailed to the publisher or vendor, but it is projected that it will be possible to place orders online. The standards on which online ordering would ideally be based are unlikely to be developed before mid-1983.

The acquisitions system is designed to eliminate all filing related to the process, to generate orders on demand, to provide accounting information and to provide access to the file by all staff.

NOTIS

NOTIS III is a comprehensive library materials management system developed by the Northwestern University Library. The first version of the software was completed in 1970 and two major revisions had been accomplished by late 1981. NOTIS includes acquisitions, processing, serials and circulation control modules. All functions are fully integrated.

In technical services, system use begins as early as receipt of an order request, with a search of the NOTIS data base. Northwestern's practice is to capture authoritative bibliographic data, when available, at the earliest possible moment. To this end, the library has a search department responsible for both preorder and precataloging verification. This department attempts to fulfill preorder and precataloging requirements prior to the placing of an order for newly requested titles.

The starting point in any search is the library's online data base. If no record is found in the NOTIS file, the operator initiates a search of the MARC data base, unless the item is unquestionably out of MARC scope. The NOTIS system maintains the complete MARC and COMARC files offline, searching them each night and retrieving the most current records the following day, and older records according to a regular schedule. An interface to the Research Libraries Information Network (RLIN) is being developed for libraries that require access to a bibliographic utility's data base.

After the transfer of data from MARC tapes into the online system, or input from other sources such as Library of Congress (LC) or National Union Catalog (NUC) copy, or the entry of provisional data, the basic bibliographic record—with appropriate modifications—is used for the production of all hardcopy output, from purchase orders through catalog cards and punched circulation cards.

The technical services subsystem operates in two modes: bibliographic and order. Each requires a different password and, although all data may be displayed in either mode, modification in the order mode is only permitted by operators with an appropriate sign-on code.

The top line of the computer screen serves as the "request line" on which the terminal operator enters the appropriate command. The system automatically displays the most common commands, but these may be overridden at any time by the operator.

In both modes the indexes provide the major access points when the bibliographic record is unknown. All name entries, whether main or added entries, and all title entries, including generic records, are created. The main entry and main title fields cause immediate online update of the indexes. Other indexed fields in the bibliographic record, such as name and title added entries, result in batched offline updating at periodic intervals. Corporate name entries appear in both normal and rotated forms for ease of access to the lowest level in the corporate hierarchy.

Three types of screen displays are possible in the bibliographic mode: full bibliographic data, copy holdings and volume holdings. On the bibliographic data screen, the fixed fields are formatted at the top and the variable data fields, headed with MARC mnemonic tags, display in MARC numeric order below. To create a new record in the proper format, the operator keys in a command indicating which of the MARC formats is to be used.

It is possible to generate a purchase order after the provisional bibliographic data and location/copy designation have been entered, regardless of whether or not a MARC transfer has occurred. In the order mode an operator inputs the appropriate vendor information, including any special instructions, and calls for printing of a purchase order. The bibliographic record number in conjunction with an order sequence number furnishes the purchase order number.

In the order mode, the holdings screen provides the link to all orders, with an alphabetical status code indicating if the order is open, cancelled, complete or a replacement. The operator selects the desired order number and receives a screen display that includes the brief bibliographic data, the vendor information, the copy control number and the order/payment/receipt data fields. The first of these fields, the order scope statement, indicates the order status, fund, encumbered amount and an action date for claiming purposes. Any payment statements will appear next and include the amount paid, invoice number and date, invoice control number and any necessary piece of identification. A receipt statement is used to record pieces received. For serials, a new automatic claim date is calculated based on the latest receipt statement modification date and predetermined claim interval information. Both the machine-set latest modification date and claiming action date appear on the screen.

Each night the computer generates a list of expired action dates that prompts claiming. In response to this list, an operator reviews each record and produces a claim memo by entering a statement containing an appropriate code and date. Claims can also be generated any time a gap is discerned without waiting for an action date list to prompt the claim. A wide variety of messages can be generated automatically. Approximately 50 memo-producing codes are in current use, generating claims for missing and overdue periodical issues and unsupplied monographs, requests for permission to return duplicate or imperfect items and requests for unsupplied invoices. Printed claims are produced overnight for dispatch in the following day's mail. A note statement entered in a data field in the order record is used to record vendor response as to the order status (out of stock, back ordered, etc.).

As of early 1982 the author observed keen interest in NOTIS. This interest is understandable, because NOTIS offers a more comprehensive list of features than normally available in other software packages. To summarize, the basic features are:

- preorder searching against a local data base;
- order record creation/update;
- purchase order writing;
- customized vendor correspondence (claims, cancellations, etc.);
- receipt posting;
- overdue item alerting;
- payment posting;
- commitment/expenditure reports.

The Northwestern University Library decided in 1981 that it would market NOTIS to other libraries. One system had already been sold to the National Library of Venezuela. Agreement was reached in 1981 with the University of Florida Library to provide the system after making several enhancements, including improved circulation control, subject access, call number access, cross references in indexes and authority management. Online funds control may also be included at some time in the future.

NOTIS software can be run on any computer which will support a standard IBM/370 operating system.

CONCLUSION

The ideal system is not currently available from any vendor. The cost of in-house development is prohibitive, often several hundred thousand dollars. Libraries that have electronic data processing expertise available can purchase a software package and adapt it to their unique needs. The library would then have to undertake ongoing software maintenance and enhancement. The cost for this may be high and unpredictable. Libraries that can afford to wait or that can accept less than the ideal system might be well-advised to do so.

6
Turnkey and Integrator Systems

TURNKEY SYSTEMS

There are three advantages to selecting one of the turnkey systems offered by a commercial vendor: (1) such systems have a relatively low price; (2) they can usually be installed more quickly than a custom-developed system; and (3) the system capabilities are clearly defined at the time of purchase.

From 50% to 80% of the costs of developing a computer system are incurred in systems design and programming; the balance of the cost is for hardware. The turnkey vendor is able to spread the software cost over a number of installations so that a single customer may pay as little as 3% of the software development cost. The contracted price will be all a library pays even if the vendor incurs costs that were not anticipated when the contract was signed—unless, of course, the specifications are modified after the contract is negotiated. Installation dates for turnkey systems are generally 90 to 120 days after the date of receipt of an order. All custom developments, in-house or contracted, take one to two years and are subject to slippage. Any features not available from a turnkey vendor at the time the order is placed, but which may become part of the standard system, also often take a year or more to develop. The features of a turnkey system are known when the contract is signed and its performance can usually be determined by looking at the system in one or more comparable libraries.

With a turnkey system it is not possible to extensively modify the software to meet individualized requirements. The cost of the turnkey system is kept low by developing one standard system and sharing the cost of that development among a number of libraries. The vendor assumes that the features of the system are attractive enough to appeal to a large market.

Most of the currently available turnkey systems for libraries were originally developed as circulation systems. Such companies as Cincinnati Electronics, CL Systems Inc. (CLSI),

DataPhase and Geac have recently begun marketing automated circulation systems that can be expanded into integrated library systems. For acquisitions control, some vendors sell separate acquisitions software packages. In other cases, acquisitions is considered an enhancement and the software is made available to existing customers without additional charge.

Hardware, software and operating costs are highly predictable. The frustration may come in having a system that does not have the features that the library would ideally desire. The library may find that a number of its standard procedures must be changed to fit in with the turnkey system.

One of the major costs of launching an automated system is the retrospective conversion of manual files. If existing acquisitions files are converted, the cost will average $1 per record. When the record can be used to support several functions, the cost can be allocated among them.

The effect of several functions sharing a data base can be illustrated as follows. According to a detailed study by King Research, an online catalog is more expensive than a card catalog over a five-year period.[1] The analysis showed that for a library with just under 500,000 titles the five-year cost of maintaining a card catalog averaged $1,263,000 while an online catalog would cost $1,506,000. The single most significant reason for the cost difference was the initial conversion of the records to machine-readable form—then calculated at $.72 for each record. Had only half the cost of creating the data been charged to the online catalog function and the other half to another function, and had the time for amortizing the equipment been extended from five to seven years, cost savings could have been demonstrated.

As no academic library has yet put its entire catalog and other functions online, there are no "real" figures against which to compare these estimates. It would appear, however, that integrated, multi-function systems will be cost-effective in the future because the retrospective conversion costs would be allocated among several functions. If the hardware is chosen wisely, a seven year amortization will be possible.

INTEGRATORS

The term "integrator" rather loosely describes a vendor that offers a variety of hardware and software services. A customer, therefore, has a single source for both. Most firms of this type began as either hardware manufacturers or dealers, or as software houses. The integrator assumes responsibility for properly matching hardware and software to one another. If the integrator is hardware-oriented, the software is likely to consist of standard packages. If the integrator has a software orientation, it will probably offer to modify standard packages or to undertake custom software development. In the library marketplace IBM is increasingly functioning as an integrator, although it continues to clearly separate the prices of its hardware and software.

The integrator, unlike the software house, often offers ongoing support for the automated system at a firm price, quoted at the time of the original purchase. At least one integrator, Sigma Data, supplements its services with a time-sharing service so that customers can share their computer and software with others that have similar requirements.

The cost of this semi-standard approach is moderate. The software is developed with the idea clearly in mind that it will be used by several customers. Thus, there is a limit to the number of changes in the basic software that would be made for any one customer.

SHARING A SYSTEM

Prior to the late 1970s, minicomputers had limited processing power. Therefore, most libraries chose to acquire stand-alone systems that served only one library. By 1978 a number of libraries had begun to share automated library systems. One of the most successful shared systems is that of the North Suburban Library System in metropolitan Chicago. Twenty-two libraries share computer resources, with some of the members paying as little as $600 per month for a single terminal, access to the shared bibliographic files, storage space for copy specific and patron information, and printing facilities generating notices and reports. Several hundred libraries in Illinois, Connecticut and other states have installed similar shared systems.

Sharing is not always cost-effective. Telecommunications costs can rapidly offset and exceed the capital cost of duplicating the system at separate locations. According to various offices of American Telephone and Telegraph, the rates for dedicated lines within a state are usually from $4 to $10 per mile per month. Using an average charge of $7 per mile per month, the cost of connecting ten terminals to a central processing unit 30 miles away would be $2100 per month. Over a five year period this would be $126,000—an amount that would almost pay for the duplication of the central site hardware and software. While it is possible to reduce ongoing telecommunications costs by linking multiple terminals to a line, this increases the capital and maintenance costs for multiplexers and other telecommunications hardware.

There are economic benefits when two or more libraries within 30 or so miles of each other share a computer system. There can also be significant service benefits. When the libraries have complementary collections and a history of interlibrary lending and reciprocal borrowing, the sharing of the data base can facilitate and strengthen these services.

Libraries considering shared systems must be sure to determine that they can specify different order formats, automatic cancellation periods, reports, etc.

There are important governance issues to be addressed when libraries share a system. First, it must be decided whether the libraries are equal partners or whether one institution owns the system and sells services to the others. If they are equal partners, committees must be established to determine such issues as what bibliographic standards will prevail, what rates will be charged to participants and how any decisions about the expansion of system capabilities will be reached. In a multi-library situation, the decision-making process is likely to be time-consuming—often requiring two or more years to select, procure and implement a system when more than five institutions are involved.

AVAILABLE SYSTEMS

This chapter describes the acquisitions systems of the major turnkey vendors and integrators. The criteria for inclusion were an existing customer base of at least six libraries and an assurance that the company would be able to deliver an automated acquisitions system in 1982.

The information in this chapter is current as of early 1982, but changes are being made so rapidly that no library should use the information for anything more than reducing the range of options to a more manageable number. A careful comparison of the most attractive remaining options should then be made using the library's own specifications or checklist of requirements. The checklist in Chapter 5 can be used as a starting point.

CINCINNATI ELECTRONICS (CE)
2630 Glendale–Milford Rd.
Cincinnati, OH 45241
(513) 563-6000

Although originally scheduled for completion in mid-1980, Cincinnati Electronics' integrated library automated system—CLASSIC—had not been installed and accepted in any library by early 1982. Company spokesmen attributed the delay to the demand for the installation of circulation systems and the need to undertake more modification of the purchased software than had originally been anticipated.

The CLASSIC acquisitions subsystem is designed to handle all ordering and accounting functions. The vendor's stated objective is to streamline the acquisition process by virtually eliminating paperwork, hard copy files and the duplication of orders. It also seeks to provide improvements in accounting by offering ready access to various data formats, unified methods of handling all types of transactions and greater accuracy in transactions.

The system handles regular book orders, orders for local, state, federal and international documents, manuscripts, audiovisual materials and equipment, initial serial orders, art prints, etc. It also accommodates the acquisition of gifts and exchanges.

CLASSIC is interactive and online. The acquisitions program was originally written in COBOL by the Duke University Library, where it has been operational for over four years. While the acquisitions system may be operated as a stand-alone function, it is being redesigned to perform as a functional entity of a totally integrated library information system with direct interface to circulation and other functions. The interface between acquisitions and circulation will allow reserves to be placed against items still in the purchasing process.

Acquisitions Functions

If a library uses OCLC or has access to any other bibliographic data base for pre-order searching, any matches may be recorded on cassette tape through an offline interface. The complete title records may then be loaded directly into the acquisitions system data base, thus eliminating handkeying of the data. Only library-specific information need be entered manually. This may include the number of copies to be ordered, the price per copy, the fund to be encumbered, vendor information, order date, publishing date (if it is a prepublication order) and any special instructions for routing, cataloging and processing.

After all the order information and the date of order have been entered into the system, a purchase order to the desired vendor will be automatically generated. Purchase orders may be generated at will or when the daily notices are produced. The specified fund will be encumbered immediately.

When an order is received, the material is checked in on the system and the accounts are automatically adjusted, moving funds from encumbrance to paid out status. The invoice number and the amount are kept together in the system until a check is written to the appropriate vendor. If the price of some item has changed since the time of order, the price field in the order record may be updated. The funds will then be automatically adjusted. If the item ordered is not received within a specified period, a claims notice will be generated to be sent to the vendor, unless some notification of delay has been received and noted on the system.

When a book is checked into the system, a routing indicator may be displayed or printed showing the final destination of the specific copy, cataloging instructions or processing instructions.

The check writing function is run as a background process at times specified by the library. Up to 21 order transactions with a vendor may be incorporated in one check. The check stub will include the invoice number of each transaction covered by that check. The check writing function is optional. For those libraries not performing this function, vouchers may be printed for forwarding to the department responsible for paying the library's bills.

If the book has to be returned to the vendor for some reason, the order record may be updated to include the reason for the return. The date returned and the date of the reorder will also be added. If an order has been put on a waiting list by the vendor or publisher because the material is temporarily out of print or out of stock, the reason for the delay may also be entered on the order record, together with information such as the date of vendor's notification and the expected date of shipment. When an order has been cancelled by a publisher or vendor, the reason for the cancellation and the date may be entered on the record and a new order to a second vendor established. The system can keep track of several different vendors for an item.

In all cases, the original order information remains in the system. This way, a complete and up-to-date history is available for any order until it is either finally cancelled or received. Interaction between the acquisitions and circulation systems enables patrons to be informed of the status of the order and the approximate date that the material will be available.

Under normal circumstances, the system will not allow an operator to over-encumber a fund. It will notify the operator that the fund does not have enough money to cover the price of the item. In this situation, it is possible to do one of two things: the operator may predate the purchase order so that it will not be generated until the fund is replenished; or, if the operator has the proper authority, the fund may be over-encumbered.

If, for some reason, the material is not to be ordered, the title record can be entered (in part or in full) together with the reason for not ordering it. This may be of interest at some later date if the material is requested again.

Cooperative Acquisitions and Standing Orders

The CLASSIC system also allows for cooperative acquisitions. If the library is a member of a consortium, the individual library can search the data bases of the member libraries before placing an order. If the item is part of a member's collection, the individual library can decide whether to order its own copy of the item. If the library chooses not to order, the reason can be noted on the computer record together with the nearest location from which the item can be borrowed. This record can be maintained in the data base to accommodate future requests from patrons for the same item.

If the library has an online catalog or an online circulation system, acquisitions records can be queried from any terminal. Patrons and staff can access the acquisitions record from any public service area and determine the on-order status of an item.

Standing orders must be treated differently from regular orders because funds cannot be encumbered when prices are not known. The order information may be entered and the standing purchase order transmitted. As the material in a series and the bill for it are received, the price can be entered into the system. The funds are then immediately transferred to the "paid out" column for the particular fund involved.

Gifts and Exchange Items

The acquisition of gifts is handled differently because funds are not encumbered. First, a search is made to determine if the gift duplicates something already in the collection. If so, and the gift is to become an added copy, the only information that need be entered is receipt of the gift, the donor's name, agency location, destination and other cataloging and processing instructions. The gift is then checked in, a routing slip produced and the material delivered for cataloging as an added copy.

If the gift is not a duplicate, a record must be created before the item is checked in and routed to cataloging. The record is established in the same way as a regular order with the exception of encumbrance and generation of a purchase order. The system will also keep a record of all gifts received over a period of time. A report may be generated upon demand; a list of donors may also be produced, showing the materials donated, the type of materials donated and the approximate value of the donations. The library may also print receipts for donors wishing to deduct the gift from their income tax. Receipts can be generated once a year (around tax time) or on demand.

An exchange item, when received, is handled in much the same way as a gift. Instead of entering donor information, details of the exchange institution are recorded. Not only can the system keep track of the materials received on exchange but it will also keep a running account of materials that are sent on exchange. The program will accommodate such information as when a particular item was sent, the number of copies, and, for series and annuals, the number of volumes the receiving institution has been sent. When the library receives materials it wishes to send as exchange items, it may search the data base to produce a list of institutions that have received previous issues or volumes of a particular title. It is then a simple procedure to print this list or address labels for dispatching the items.

Serials

Orders for new serials are handled similarly to orders for other materials. The order information, subscription price, subscription agency, subscription expiration date and the destination location are entered. A subscription order is generated for dispatch to the appropriate subscription agency and the appropriate funds are encumbered. When the first issue is received, it is checked in against the order record and sent on to the serials department. Subsequent issues are sent directly to the serials department for manual check in. A serials check-in system is being developed which will handle this procedure automatically. For those serials ordered directly, a report may be generated periodically to notify the library when to renew the subscriptions.

Reports

Continuously updated reports of the acquisitions procedures are available to the library. These reports may be accessed online or printed out. If desired, on-order cards can also be printed for filing in the card catalog. If the library maintains an online catalog, the order record can be added to the catalog.

Reports available on CLASSIC include:

Listing of vendors by accession number and name
Account transaction detail
Encumbrance trial balance by vendor
Encumbrance trial balance by order number
Operating expenses for fiscal year
Fee fund
Fund balances
Libraries' Accounts Payable Distribution Register
Credit balance listing
Items on-order
Monographs on-order
Serials on-order

Items on-order by fund
Items on-order by department
Items on-order by professor
Donor list—alphabetical, by type of material
Donor receipts
Items received on exchange
Items sent on exchange
List of standing orders

Costs

The software is designed to run on the Univac V77 line of minicomputers—a family of modular machines consisting of the models 200, 400, 500, 600, 700 and 800. Primary memory ranges from 16K to 2048K bytes and disk capacity to 1600 Megabytes. The system is particularly easy to expand.

A library choosing the Cincinnati Electronics acquisitions system could purchase both the software and the hardware or, if hardware had previously been acquired for the CE circulation system, software only. The price for the CLASSIC acquisitions software had not been determined by late fall, 1981, but it was projected at $20,000.

CL SYSTEMS INC. (CLSI)
81 Norwood Ave.
Newton, MA 02160
(617) 965-6310

CLSI's first product, introduced in the early 1970s, was an online book acquisitions system. Because of changes in library requirements for automation in the late 1970s, CLSI shifted its emphasis to a circulation control package and an online catalog capability. The system is known as LIBS 100. CLSI is now developing and integrating a new acquisitions system with the existing circulation control and public access products. The acquisitions software package was being tested in early 1982.

CLSI usually bids the Digital Equipment Corp. (DEC) PDP 11/34 minicomputer, a very small mini that can be expanded to only 256K bytes of primary memory. It is, therefore, easy to saturate a CLSI system. At the present time, the only way to increase processing capability is to wire two or more PDP 11/34s together.

The acquisitions module shares the central files of CLSI's LIBS 100 system with the other modules. It includes functions for ordering, reviewing, claiming, cancelling and routing materials; producing management reports; maintaining vendor and fund accounts, and producing financial reports.

Acquisitions Functions

LIBS 100 allows the library to specify the content of the bibliographic record and up to 30 search keys for the bibliographic file. Any of these search keys can be used for searching the bibliographic file, which is internally linked with the item (copy) records in the locator file. Thus, a pre-order search not only retrieves bibliographic information about the title, but also immediately displays information regarding the whereabouts of each item on order, in process, in the collection or in circulation.

The library may establish lists of collections ordering materials, with a default payment fund associated with each collection. The list can also specify the location of the collections—adult, juvenile, circulation or reference. The system will accommodate different order types such as rush or normal, the payment type (prepaid or regular), the vendor and the shipping instructions.

Prior to ordering, the bibliographic file is searched by using any of the bibliographic search keys. If the bibliographic record is not on file, a new record is entered. When the record has been identified and/or entered, the system will display the first collection in the previously established list. If a list has not been previously established, the operator may enter a valid collection ID. The system will then display the default fund and location indicators, the total number of items in the collection or in process, and the total number of on-order items for that collection. An order quantity is entered and the system then leads the operator through the ordering list, requesting that a quantity for each collection be specified.

As orders are entered, the system immediately updates the encumbrance. It compares the resulting encumbrance with a library-defined early warning factor; if an order results in the near depletion of a fund, the system will display a warning to the operator.

At any point, the operator may escape from the list, enter a new collection identifier and the quantity for that collection, or re-enter the list and correct previous information. When the system reaches the end of the predefined list, it gives the operator the opportunity to enter another collection, to re-enter the list or to specify another title and repeat the process for that title. The operator may also exit from the order process at this point.

As orders are processed, the system will automatically perform a number of file updates, ensuring that all orders to one vendor are printed together, quantities are accumulated for order purposes, title records are added or updated for all modules, a claiming date is established, and the proper funds are encumbered.

Purchase orders may be printed on demand. In this process the library may select all purchase orders, a specific purchase order number or the purchase orders for a particular vendor. Orders may also be printed by payment type or order type.

When books are received, they are compared with the packing slip and/or a copy of the vendor's invoice. Any missing, damaged or unacceptable books are noted on this document and entered into the system.

The order and bibliographic files may be searched in a number of different ways. If the vendor has included the library's purchase order number on its invoice or packing slip, the number may be entered to recall the purchase order line-by-line. The purchase order may also be searched using the bibliographic key. The system will then display title and order information, and the operator can enter the quantity received, price information, the shorts (items missing from the order) and information about damaged items.

If the library's purchase order number is not available with the shipment, on-order information can be accessed using vendor or bibliographic keys. As in the alternate access modes, when on-order information is found, the record is updated by addition of received quantity, price information, shorts and damage quantities.

Gifts and Other Items

If the material received is a gift or some other item which has not been specifically ordered—material on a package rental program, for instance—the accession process is similar to the order check-in procedure described above. In this case, the operator specifies which account is to be debited. The library may also enter the collections to which the received copies are to be allocated. New title information may also be recorded in the bibliographic file at this time. The system automatically performs all of the file updates described previously in the order process, as well as other file updates specified in the receipt process. These updates ensure that encumbrances are adjusted, vendor records are kept current, bibliographic and copy information reflect ownership, and order and claiming records are changed.

If a vendor responds to an order or a claim notice with information such as "temporarily out of print," the library may decide to cancel the order. The entry of this information into the system generates a cancel notice to be sent to the vendor, and the revised information will appear on an on-order status report to each ordering collection. If the order is not cancelled, then the information will appear on the general on-order status report, but not on the report to the ordering collection.

Routing

The library may specify the contents of a number of different routing slips: to binding, to cataloging, to a hold area, to final processing or to approval.

The CLSI system automatically determines whether the books have to go to binding or to approval by examining files to see if these indicators have been set. If they have not been set, the system examines the bibliographic file to see if the book has been cataloged. If it has, the system then routes the book to final processing. But if a copy is still in cataloging, the system produces the routing slip for the hold area. If the book has not been cataloged and there is no copy in cataloging, the system routes the first copy received to cataloging and subsequent copies to the hold area. The routing slips contain library-designated text as well as information showing to which collection the copies are allocated.

To facilitate and monitor this routing process, the library may install laser or hand-held wand devices throughout the processing area and affix a bar-code label to each item as it is checked in. As the book moves from one part of the processing area to another, the book can be checked to the new area. In this manner, the location of any book can be determined at any moment, and notices can be generated automatically when a book has remained in one area more than a specified period of time. Lists of these items can also be generated.

Claims and Cancellation

The library may invoke the claiming process on demand. The appropriate files are scanned to determine all items which have not been received within a specified period. The system then prints claim notices to the vendors, with items grouped by vendor.

The CLSI system accommodates both automatic cancellation of items not received in a library-specified period and operator-initiated cancellations. The cancellation notices to vendors are formatted by the library with library-designated messages. At the same time, the system generates a list, by library collection, indicating which items have been cancelled. In addition, the system maintains a record of the cancellations in the vendor file, so that a vendor's performance can be evaluated.

Reports

The system can also produce a vendor performance report showing, for each vendor, the total dollar amount of materials received, the number of items ordered from that vendor, the percentage of fulfillment, the average number of days from order to receipt and the average discount.

Summary reports showing the appropriation, the encumbrance, the unencumbered balance, total debit, total credits and the balance for each fund can also be produced on demand. This information may be repeated twice for each fund, allowing for periods when books are still being received from orders placed against the previous years' appropriation.

The system will also produce a variety of statistical reports showing the number of items and/or titles acquired in library-specified parts of each collection over a library-defined period of time.

Financial adjustments to debit a fund and credit a vendor, or to credit a fund and debit the vendor, may be made online. Each adjustment causes the appropriate debit or credit memo entry to be made in the debit/credit file, and inserts a line into the vendor's statement file, cross-referencing the debit or credit memo. In addition, the system will produce, on demand, checks or vouchers and statements for each vendor. These statements itemize each debit and credit transaction posted to the vendor's account.

Other Features

Because the book acquisitions module accesses the same bibliographic data base that is used by circulation control and the public access catalog, all bibliographic records are library-specified with variable length fields. Using existing interface capabilities, MARC records can be entered and used for acquisitions functions.

Any LIBS 100 keyboard/display and composite terminals can be used for book acquisitions functions. The LIBS 100 terminal display printer may be used for the printing of routing slips and other short reports. Longer reports and notices may be printed at any of the console medium- or high-speed printers.

LIBS 100 provides password security to control access to on-order, fund and vendor information, as well as to various book acquisitions processes. The system can prevent the display of fund and vendor account information to unauthorized operators. Password security applies to the use of book acquisitions processes such as ORDER, RECEIPT, CLAIM, CANCEL, etc.

Costs

The company has bid the acquisitions module separately for $20,000. As part of a software package containing several functions for a combined cost, the acquisitions software price may be estimated at approximately $10,000.

DATAPHASE SYSTEMS INC.
3770 Broadway
Kansas City, MO 64111
(816) 931-7927

As of late 1981 the DataPhase acquisitions system was still in a rudimentary stage of development, although the projected date of completion had been the summer of 1980. In late 1981 the projected completion date was moved to mid-1982, and a pilot test in the Atlanta Public Library was underway in spring 1982.

A major factor in DataPhase's delays appears to be its commitment to rewrite all of the software for its ALIS library system to a second generation designated as ALIS II. The second generation system is designed to have the advantage of a new operating system and greater flexibility than ALIS I. Both run on Data General hardware. The most commonly bid machines are the Eclipse S/140 and the S/250. The latter can be expanded to more than 2 Megabytes of primary memory. A larger system known as the ALIS IIe runs on Tandem computers.

Acquisitions Functions

The acquisitions function will use the same data base as circulation and cataloging and will be accessible from the same terminals. The objective is a fully integrated stand-alone automated library information system. Files will be updated online as new information about a title on order is acquired. A person at any terminal in the system will be able to determine the current status of all titles ordered or received by the library. Once an acquisitions record is created, all further information, whether from the acquisitions department or later on from cataloging, is treated as an update to this record—no rekeying is required for any information already available in the system.

The acquisitions file consists of acquisitions records for each title a library has on order or has received. To ensure ease of use, the access points included purchase order number, main entry, title, LC card number, ISBN/ISSN and bibliographic record vendor number. The acquisitions file includes information on bibliographic data, acquisitions type, status, branch/copy/fund, invoices, vendors, accounting, control and vendor reports.

The acquisitions function components will vary according to individual library requirements. The acquisitions type assigned to each acquisitions record is an important element. Currently, the following acquisitions types are being planned: new order, selection list, gift, exchange, on approval, standing order, blanket order, continuation, U.S. Government document, library-specific type #1, library-specific type #2.

Depending upon the acquisitions type a user selects, the system response will vary. The screen may show:

1) The prompts for bibliographic information to be entered or transferred from elsewhere in the system.

2) The prompts for other order data.

3) Whether or not a purchase order needs to be produced.

4) The information that appears on a purchase order.

5) The claim cycle for the order. (An operator can override the system claim cycle established for each vendor.)

Status Information

In addition to acquisitions type, another key element in each acquisitions record is the status information. Status information is cumulative—each new status is added to an existing status list to give a history of the order. The information includes current status, the date that status was set and a free-text message describing the status. Examples of statuses currently planned include: received partial, received complete, reported, returned partial, invoice received, etc.

The status indicator provides information both to library users who want to determine the current state of an order, and also to the system which will use the data to initiate a variety of activities such as producing printouts, deleting orders or producing open order reports.

Bibliographic Information

Bibliographic information for titles to be ordered can originate from several processes within a library:

1) New orders: Bibliographic information for new orders will be entered into the system using a formatted screen. The system will use mnemonic prompts to request a user to enter the appropriate information; internally, the bibliographic information will be translated into the MARC format to make the acquisitions records compatible with other bibliographic records in the data base.

   If a library belongs to a cataloging utility such as OCLC, it will be able to request on order titles from OCLC and load them into the circulation system data base. Appropriate bibliographic information can then be automatically transferred from the circulation data base to the acquisitions record. No additional keying of bibliographic information will be required.

2) Selection lists: Selection lists for titles the library intends to order will be kept online on the system. These lists allow branch libraries to indicate their choice of titles, along with the number of copies they wish to order. When titles from the selection list are ready for ordering, the system will transfer bibliographic information already available on the selection list to the acquisitions record. Again, no duplicate keying of bibliographic information will be required.

3) Added copies: Bibliographic information for added or replacement copies is taken from the ALIS data base record.

4) Received titles: For firm orders, the operator will retrieve the record already in the system. For libraries using vendor approval plans, bibliographic information for an approval plan title is entered when the title is received in the library.

Once the bibliographic information has been established, the system will prompt for other order data required in an acquisitions record. Upon completion of an acquisitions record, it will be filed both in the acquisitions file and in the full ALIS data base. A temporary copy record will be created for each copy ordered. Both the ALIS title and copy records will be accessible using the standard ALIS inquiry routines.

Purchase Orders

Not all of the acquisitions types that can be accommodated require purchase orders. For those that do, purchase orders will be produced using batch printing routines. There will be one purchase order per title record ordered. Procedures involved in printing purchase orders include updating the vendor file, updating encumbrances in the fund file, sorting the purchase orders in vendor order, and producing the purchase orders themselves. Purchase orders may be output on paper forms or on computer tape.

When ordered titles are received, an operator will retrieve the acquisitions record to verify the correctness and completeness of the order. A variety of receiving statuses, plus a free-text message that can be appended to each one, will allow the precise indication of the disposition of the items received. For titles received without purchase orders—approval plan materials, standing orders, etc.—an acquisitions record will be created upon receipt so that the order can be tracked through the later stages of acquisitions (such as fund expenditures, invoicing and reports generation).

As described earlier, when the acquisitions record is first created a title record and one copy record for each copy ordered is added to the full ALIS data base. Part of the receiving procedure involves the addition of an item label to the item(s) received; internally, the system will replace each copy record with a permanent record tied to the label number. The status displayed in regular ALIS inquiry will automatically change from "ON ORDER" to "IN PROCESS." Invoice information and vendor reports are also added to the acquisitions record. Other procedures entailed in receiving titles include updating the vendor file and various other files.

Vendor File

The vendor file is created and maintained online. A formatted screen will prompt an operator for required vendor information. The vendor file can be printed for a hard-copy listing of all vendors used by the library. Records on the file are accessible by either vendor name or number.

In addition to vendor name and address, the vendor file includes a claim cycle established by the library to indicate when claims should be produced by the system. This automatic cycle can be overridden for individual purchase orders. It also includes vendor performance statistics, maintained and calculated by the system, that tell the library the average amount of time a particular vendor requires to fill an order.

Current plans are for the acquisitions function to handle several methods of payment, including payment on the invoice, prepayment, standing order, continuation, cash, deposit account and coupons.

Fund File

The fund file will allow for up to four levels of fund "nesting." The file is created and maintained online. Most updating of the file occurs automatically, as a result of orders being placed (funds encumbered) or orders received (funds debited). For each fund, the information stored includes the amounts budgeted, encumbered, expended and available. Because the file is updated online as transactions occur, the fund file is always up-to-date. For example, the system will automatically notify an operator who is creating a new purchase order if the funds requested exceed the funds available in a particular allocation.

Reports and Other Features

Output planned for the acquisitions function includes: new or revised purchase orders, claim letters, selection lists, multi-part work document, new books report, vendor lists, open order report and fund status report.

The acquisitions function will complement the ALIS circulation system in several ways:

1) Data base searching: Since the acquisitions record is also accessible in the full ALIS data base, it can be inspected from any terminal in the system.

2) Holds: Patrons can place holds for items on order or in process. When the status of these items changes to "shelf" when processing is concluded, operators are alerted to place the items on the hold shelf, and patrons are automatically sent hold availability notices.

3) Collection usage: The ALIS circulation system provides a series of reports that indicate collection usage. A purchase alert report also tells the library when the number of holds on a title exceeds a library-specified threshold. This information can be used to help formulate acquisitions and collection development policies.

Acquisitions records are created within the structure of the MARC format. When a title is ready for full cataloging, minimal acquisitions records can be upgraded using the ALIS master holdings maintenance function. Alternatively, if a library belongs to a cataloging utility such as OCLC, full cataloging records can be requested from the utility's data base to update the acquisitions record.

Costs

The company has bid its circulation systems with the promise that the acquisitions module will be available to the library as a subsequent software release at no extra cost. The total software price for the entire ALIS system is usually bid at $40,000, plus $15,000 in software license fees. Sixty libraries had purchased DataPhase systems by early 1982.

GEAC LTD.
350 Steelcase Rd. West
Markham, Ontario, L3R1B3, Canada
(416) 475-0525

The Geac budget to develop an acquisitions system was approved on July 1, 1980. An "options document" was circulated to prospective customers in an attempt to determine what modifications should be made to the acquisitions system developed by the Guelph University Library (the system ran on Geac equipment). The hardware used would be the same Geac 6000 and 8000 minicomputers previously available for circulation control, but now designated to support integrated systems. The 8000 is a multi-processor system which can be expanded to more than 2 Megabytes of primary memory.

Geac assumed that changes would be relatively minor and that the first non-Guelph customer would have an operating system by the first quarter of 1981. Several of Geac's 18 circulation systems users were expected to adopt the acquisitions system. As with all other vendors, development fell behind schedule and in early 1982 no acquisitions system was operational.

Libraries sharing the Geac circulation system were particularly concerned that the design of the Guelph system did not provide separate system parameters for different libraries.

Acquisitions Functions

The acquisitions module of the Geac Library Information System is an integrated data base management system capable of handling all types of purchasing requirements for public, academic and corporate libraries. The comprehensive acquisitions system allows up-to-the-minute detailing of fund accounting, ordering activity, invoicing, receiving, searching and currency control. Each function of the system is made available only to those people with the appropriate authorization. The acquisitions system is available as a stand-alone module, or as an integrated component of the Geac Library Information System (which includes circulation).

Ordering

The ordering routine allows the user to assemble all the information required to describe the requested item and print a purchase order. Vendor selection is part of this process, but this function is available only to authorized acquisitions personnel. An order may be assigned to one or many fund accounts, allowing shared costing. This facility allows very complex orders to be defined and will handle many types of orders such as rush, rush search, continuations, standing orders, confirmation orders, gifts, no cost orders, prepaid orders, multivolume/multi-copy orders and others. When a request for material is generated, the cost is assessed to the fund account(s) and vendor record for that order. This cost is logically updated whenever the currency changes, the cost is updated, the order is received (either in whole or in part) or the invoice is paid.

Fund Accounting

Fund accounting is an online function enabling acquisitions personnel to set up and report fund statuses. Each order is attached to one or many fund accounts within the system. Appropriate checks are in place to stop a fund from being overrun without proper authorization. Any fund account that is approaching an overspent condition is reported to library management via a daily report, and further spending against a fund may be precluded for all or selected types of orders.

Each invoice is recorded in the acquisitions module, and is accessible by the vendor's own invoice number. Totals for net, gross, taxes, handling charges and discount amounts are maintained and checked automatically. Invoices may be paid by check, money order, cash or internal transfer, and a complete reconciliation function is supplied.

Receiving

The receiving function features complete check in with error checking against both orders and invoices. The terminal operator is notified of various routing options that may be assigned to a receipt so that received material is sent quickly to the specific cataloging location and/or requesting agency.

Bibliographic Search

Bibliographic searching for pre-order search or search-on-arrival requirements is available. The operator may search all bibliographic files to ascertain the existence of an item and use that information in the ordering process.

The currency control feature of the acquisitions module allows the automatic revaluation of orders for which no payment has yet been made. This causes the budgetary position to reflect changing currency rates at all times. Materials may be ordered in one currency and paid for in another.

Reports

The system produces reports overnight, without the presence of a computer operator, which are held until the following day for printing. At this time, any number of copies may be printed. These reports may occur as part of a regular operation, or as a special, once-only, request. The following is a list of available reports:

- purchase orders
- vendor statistics
- short shipment notices
- order action lists
- agency status reports
- fund accounting reports
- claiming notices
- management statistics
- checks and money orders
- MARC tape profiles

Other Features

Other system features include vendor control and data transfer from the National Library of Canada MARC update tape service. Vendor information is accessible by vendor name or vendor code and includes statistical data for each vendor. Information such as the amount of time required to deliver material, total amounts spent (cumulative and year-to-date) and vendor performance levels is also available.

Costs

The cost of the Geac acquisitions module is tentatively fixed at $20,000, although the company has bid a multi-function system package at a discount to some libraries.

M/ACOM SIGMA DATA INC.
5515 Security Lane
Rockville, MD 20852
(301) 984-3636

Sigma Data's DATALIB is an integrated library system that includes acquisitions. It is run on the Data General Eclipse line of minicomputers, usually the S/150 or the S/250. This is the same equipment line used by DataPhase. When DATALIB was introduced, it was not a turnkey system; rather, it was specifically designed to meet the particular needs of a group of federal libraries. The system began with acquisitions and has recently added cataloging and circulation control. The latter does not use machine-readable labels, but requires keying of all patron and item numbers. Sigma Data is now marketing to other special libraries, but it continues to use the customized system approach because it believes that the customer's parent organization will insist on conformity to existing internal procedures. The company can best be described as an integrator of hardware and software.

Sigma Data does not support the MARC II communications format—a decision that reflects its history as a vendor to special libraries with collections of limited size.

While three stand-alone systems have been sold, to the Executive Office of the President, the Department of Justice Library and the Texaco corporate library, the majority of customers have chosen to share a system which Sigma Data has installed at its office. This service bureau approach relieves the libraries of any computer management responsibilities. In early 1982 there were six libraries using this service bureau system, all of them federal libraries. They shared a Data General Eclipse M/600 operated by Sigma Data at its Rockville, MD, service center.

The greatest strength of the Sigma Data system is in the acquisition and control of technical reports. Sigma Data has no immediate plans to market to other than federal and corporate libraries; its current strategy is to use the library system as a way of selling the company's expertise in handling an organization's procurement functions for all types of supplies and equipment.

The librarians contacted were all extremely pleased with the system, but knew relatively little about it. The information in this description is, therefore based primarily on the vendor's representations and the author's personal observation.

Acquisitions Functions

The Sigma Data acquisitions system supports full ordering requirements, including the generation of purchase orders, claim and cancel notices, pending reports and fund accounting reports. The receipt/invoice function handles invoice verification, partial receipts, partial invoices and separate accounting for shipping charges. All records are in a standard variable-length record structure and the records can be transferred to tape for use on other systems.

The system is designed to use any standard ASCII terminal supporting an upper/lower case alphabet and is designed to be used by non-data processing staff in a self-tutorial mode. The four major DATALIB acquisitions functions are: file editing, file searching, order processing and report request.

File Editing

Records can be added, displayed, changed or deleted using the file editing function. There are four types of records: bibliographic, financial, vendor and consignee.

The bibliographic file is designed to be used by a single library or a network of libraries. Once the record is entered, it can be shared by all other libraries. Other libraries using the record can make modifications and their version is used for all acquisitions and cataloging activities. Up to 10 bibliographic formats can be supported for a library, each customized to the installation. The library can have one format devoted to monographs, one to journals, one to audiovisuals, and so on. The record is a variable-length, tagged structure similar to the MARC format used internationally to communicate bibliographic information. As such, MARC records can be adapted to the DATALIB format and, conversely, DATALIB records can be converted to the MARC format.

The financial file contains all the order data to support acquisitions. The order is created through the order processing function and the record can be displayed and updated through the file editing function. After the shipment has been received, certain financial data cannot be changed; this ensures that the item received is the item ordered. Although several libraries may be using DATALIB, each library has its own financial file, which is password-protected.

The vendor file contains all the addresses used to support order requirements. The address is entered once and assigned a mnemonic easily-remembered ID. When the order is prepared, the ID is entered and DATALIB prints the full address on the order. Vendor addresses can be shared with other libraries or stored as private records. Addresses can be added, changed, displayed or deleted. However, they can only be deleted if there are no pending orders using that address.

The consignee file is similar to the vendor file, except that all records are private. All "ship to" and "bill to" addresses are entered into the file, each assigned a unique ID by the library. The address is entered once and the ID is used in order preparation.

File Searching

Each file (bibliographic, financial, vendor and consignee) has specific search keys so that a record can be retrieved when the record ID is not known. The most frequently searched file is the bibliographic file, which can be searched by title, author or number. The title key is composed of the first keyword of the title followed by the first character of every word thereafter. The keyword for "The Art of Computer Programming" would be "art,ocp". Incomplete keys can be specified by use of a question mark. All items beginning with the word "art" would be retrieved with the key "art?".

The personal author key is based on the first four characters of the author's last name, the first character of the first name and (optionally) up to four characters of the first word in the title. To retrieve the above-cited title written by Donald Knuth, the author key would be "knut,d,art". To retrieve all publications written by Knuth, the key would be "knut,d?".

The corporate author key is made up of the first character of each word in the corporate author's name for up to nine words followed by the first character of the first five words in the title. Two components are separated by a slash. As an example, if Mitre Corp., Information Systems Division, published a *Directory of Automated Library Systems,* the key would be "mcisd/doals". Again, incomplete keys can be used.

There are two number keys in DATALIB. The ISBN/ISSN (or Stock Number or Originating Report Number) key is a generalized number key. If the publication has an International Standard Book Number (ISBN) or an International Standard Serial Number (ISSN), this number is the searchable key. If neither exists, but the item has a national clearinghouse stock number (such as a Government Printing Office number), that is the key. If neither of the above exists, but an originating report number identifies the document, this becomes the searchable key. The second number key is the Library of Congress card number, which is a commonly recognized number printed on the reverse of the title page in most books.

The financial file is searched by purchase order number. Either the full number or a partial number can be entered. DATALIB responds by displaying the status of each item within the order. The status information includes the quantity ordered, pending, received and invoiced, and brief bibliographic data along with any special status notes (e.g., temporarily out of stock, delayed shipment, etc.).

The vendor file is searched by vendor name. The key is based on the first word of the vendor's name followed by the first character of every word thereafter. If Sigma Data Computing Corp. were a publisher, the key would be "sigma,dcc". Incomplete keys can be entered.

The consignee file is searched by department name. As there may be several consignee records representing a parent organization, this key is constructed at the suborganizational level. For example, the "Technical Information Center" of Mitre Corp. has the key "technical,ic" while the "Personnel Department" has the key "personnel,d".

Once a record is retrieved from any of the files, it may be displayed, changed or deleted. If the search retrieves no records, one may be immediately added.

Order Processing

Six functions are supported via order processing. The new order option allows the user to create the initial order. The existing order option supports claims, cancels, update of status information and so on. The receipt, invoice and receipt/invoice options support all full and partial receipt issuing and invoicing requirements. The transfer option provides the mechanism whereby records can be moved from DATALIB to another computer environment.

Within the new order option, the user is guided through the steps necessary to prepare an order. The first step is to establish a key for the order. This is done by entering the purchase order number, the DATALIB ID assigned to the bibliographic record to be printed on the order and the ID assigned to the consignee. If the user has already entered this order into the system, a message will be displayed. If the user does not know the bibliographic or consignee IDs, a search can be initiated, or the necessary information added to establish the bibliographic or consignee record.

The next step is to enter the "page one" information for the order. This is the type of information that does not change regardless of how many items are ordered, e.g., vendor, order date, requisition number, contract number and so on. The last step is to enter the financial information for the item being ordered, e.g., the quantity, unit price, fund to be charged, subscription dates. If there are several publications to be ordered under the same purchase order, the "page one" information is not rekeyed; the user enters only the information relating to the item. If the publication is being shipped to several different addresses, the user establishes the full order record for the first consignee, and for each additional consignee changes only the information that varies from one consignee to the next, e.g., quantity ordered, fund to be charged, etc. If the library centrally processes materials for several locations and requires separate funding records, the full order record is prepared followed by separate funding records for each location.

Special order options include the following:

• Message: A 60-character message can be printed at the top of the order. This might say "Request for Quotation," "Rush Ship Items Listed Below," and so on.

• Prepaid: The user will be prompted for the cost of the item in addition to the obligation amount. All status displays and reports will show that the item is prepaid so that proper tracking can be done. On the accounting reports, the item will show as an actual expenditure in addition to an obligation.

• Hold order: Orders may be entered but not printed until specifically released by the user. This is useful for publications that are of marginal interest and that might be ordered with end-of-year funding.

• Approval: Publications received by the library automatically and for which no order record exists (e.g., blanket purchase arrangements) are entered using the approval option, so that both order receipt and invoice information can be entered at one time.

Once an order has been printed, various follow-up actions may be required. To support these requirements, the existing order option is used. If an item has been ordered but not received in a reasonable time, a claim notice can be generated. Up to nine claims can be printed for an item. The printed notice references the original order information with an appropriate message to the vendor. To initiate a claim, the user enters the claim function and keys the ID of the record to be claimed. No other steps are required. The same procedure is used to cancel an item. A cancellation notice is printed referencing the original order information. If the vendor responds to an order explaining reasons for non-shipment, the status option can be used to enter explanatory notes. Whenever this record is displayed, the status will automatically show. The user can also reissue an order. This allows the user to amend orders, for example, when the order information stays the same, and the order price changes, or when transferring the order to another vendor.

Receipt and invoice functions can be performed when the item is received and when invoicing is received. The invoice data can be entered before or after receipt of an item. Partial or full receipting is supported. In the case of partial receipting, the remaining quantity pending can be claimed and tracked like any outstanding order. Invoicing supports a full audit trail for partially invoiced items, tracking the invoice number, account number and date along with the quantity invoiced and date paid.

DATALIB can automatically compute discounts (entered as a dollar amount or a percentage) and shipping and handling charges for all items invoiced. The user enters the unit cost for each item on the invoice, and then enters the total discount, total handling charges and total shipping charges. The shipping charges can be prorated against the unit cost for the items invoiced or stored as a separate fund account record. DATALIB prorates dicount, handling and (optionally) shipping costs against the selected invoice records and displays the total computed invoice amount. It also provides the dollar and cent discrepancy between the invoice-entered total and the system-computed total, allowing the user to change costs appropriately.

The transfer option allows the user to transfer the completed order record to standard 1600 BPI, 9 track magnetic tape. Along with the data, the user receives a basic COBOL program providing guidelines on how to read the records on other computer IBM facilities. Once a record is transferred, the user determines its disposal on the DATALIB system. It can be purged immediately, retained for one to 24 months or retained indefinitely. Generally speaking, technical report purchases are purged immediately; books are retained for one to 24 months; and serial and journal records are retained indefinitely as they must be reused in the next fiscal year.

Reports

The use of DATALIB is divided into two operational environments:

Interactive environment. During specified hours of the day, all interactive operations are performed. This includes file editing, file searching, order processing and submitting requests for reports and products.

Batch environment. During specified hours of the day, all reports and products are printed. This includes purchase orders, pending reports, accounting reports, etc.

While the hardware and software do not preclude the interactive and batch environment from running simultaneously, generally this is not done as the reports should reflect the data at the close of a given period of time. Typically, all interactive activities occur during regular business hours; during evening hours, all products are generated. Therefore, the report request function allows the library to submit requests for reports to be produced during noninteractive hours. These reports include the following:

Purchase Orders

A formal purchase order or requisition form, custom-tailored to meet the client's internal requirements, is provided. An informal purchase order, used to communicate purchase requests from agents where a contract has been established, is generally used by all clients to transmit basic order information.

Worksheets

For every record entered into DATALIB, an 8½-inch x 11-inch worksheet is produced showing all bibliographic and order information. This worksheet can be sent to off-site locations as a verification of order placement; or it can be placed in the item at the time of receipt and forwarded on to the cataloging department.

Pending Report

Sorted by title, purchase order number or status, this report tracks all transactions currently on DATALIB for the library. An aging factor indicates how long the order has been outstanding to facilitate claims review. The library can restrict the report to certain order statuses (such as keyed, ordered, claimed, cancelled, received), and ignore inactive statuses (such as hold, awaiting purge, currently inactive).

Fund Status Report

DATALIB provides two fiscal year-to-date reports. Whatever the library enters into the ''fund'' data element and the ''object class'' data element provide the basis for these reports. In addition to fund accounting, some libraries track collection growth by subject category. Federal libraries track object class information, which distinguishes monograph purchases from serial and journal purchases. Every time the report is run, the balance forward for the fund (or object class) is shown, along with all transactions occurring since the last report. Cancellations are shown with a cancel date. Three dollar amounts are maintained: order amount, pending amount and cost amount. There is a new balance forward for each fund (or object class) for each of these amounts along with a grand total.

The library may obtain a report of all journals or serials due to expire within a specific date range. This report can be sorted by title, expiration date or consignee. In the latter case, the report is customized for distribution to the consignee and is used by the library to obtain authorization for renewals.

Consignee Directory

While the library has an interactive search capability for retrieving vendor and consignee address records, the directories provide a useful adjunct to data preparation activities so that the necessary codes can be entered on the worksheet prior to keying the record into DATALIB.

Vendor Performance

Currently under development, this report statistically tracks the total number of days lapsed from the order date to the date of receipt, providing mean, standard deviation and minimum-maximum data.

Other Features

The functions that were still under development in early 1982 were deposit accounting and link to external bibliographic data bases. The former function will track purchases against a deposit account and provide fiscal year-to-date accounting similar to the fund and object class status reports. The link to external data bases will expand the bibliographic resources required by libraries by establishing a computer-to-computer link to a selected major bibliographic data base to facilitate both acquisitions and cataloging operations with DATALIB.

Costs

The cost of DATALIB is $27,000 per year to the subscribing library if Sigma Data provides its shared computing facilities. This includes unlimited access to the computer, all of the central site operating personnel, the software, a "hotline" service eight hours per day to solve problems, a messenger service, all supplies and the time required by one to two system programmers to develop new programs. The approach of Sigma Data is one of total facility management. The cost of the stand-alone minicomputer system depends upon the configuration of the system.

7

Bibliographic Utilities and Wholesalers

The primary advantage of an acquisitions system offered by a bibliographic utility or wholesaler is that it is tied to an established data base. In the case of a bibliographic utility system, the library's cataloging data base will be linked with its acquisitions records.

BIBLIOGRAPHIC UTILITY SYSTEMS

With a bibliographic utility's acquisitions system, a small library may be able to use its present cataloging terminal(s) rather than purchase new ones. Moreover, the choice of a utility's system involves a minimal capital investment for the library, even when additional terminals and modems have to be purchased. If the utility prints purchase orders centrally, no other hardware is required. If the library is to print the orders, a letter quality printer should be purchased. Because there is so little investment in hardware, it is easy for a library to discontinue use of a utility system and change to an in-house, turnkey or wholesaler system if one of the latter becomes more attractive.

The greatest potential disadvantage of bibliographic utility acquisitions systems is the transaction basis of charging. Basic fees range from $1.50 to $2.50 per item acquired. Printed forms may increase the cost per order by 50 cents. Over a five-year period a large library may spend considerably more on transaction-based charges than it would to acquire and operate a turnkey system.

In some cases, the bibliographic utilities are pursuing a distributed systems approach to acquisitions automation. That is, they are attempting to make large-scale automation effective by providing manageable networks that integrate their big computers and huge data bases with smaller in-library computers for the maintenance of local files and the processing of fund accounting and invoice preparation.

For a time the Online Computer Library Center (OCLC) appeared to be a significant exception to this approach, undertaking the development of both acquisitions and circulation on its large computer system in Columbus, OH. However, in late 1981, OCLC announced that while it would continue that development (known as the Local Library System), it would also enhance and market the Claremont Colleges system (The Total Library System) to libraries that would be better served by performing some functions locally. The planned use of OCLC's Total Library System is similar to the "maxi/mini" approach taken by UTLAS, described later in this chapter.

BOOK WHOLESALER SYSTEMS

For a number of years two major U.S. book wholesalers—Baker and Taylor, and Brodart—have been seeking to extend their activities to include automated library services. There has been a double motivation for this development: (1) to increase income directly through revenue from the automated services, and (2) to increase income indirectly through the generation of orders from libraries which may well choose to purchase their books from the supplier of the ordering system. The expansion of wholesalers' online ordering systems into automated acquisitions systems with online ordering features was a response to the development of competitive turnkey and bibliographic utility systems.

While neither vendor appears to have realized profits from the supply of automation services, company managers appear to believe that online ordering—the single most distinguishing feature of the wholesaler systems—guarantees the vendor a large percentage of the orders of libraries using its facility. The systems are designed to make ordering from the wholesaler supplying the system easier than ordering from other vendors.

From early 1981 to early 1982 the charges for wholesaler systems rose from approximately $600 per month to more than $1000 per month as the range of capabilities increased. The relatively high minimum price makes the wholesaler systems most attractive to large libraries, which can put 10,000 to 50,000 orders through a single terminal without paying the incremental $1.50 to $2.50 per order that they would face if using a bibliographic utility system. The capital investment of a turnkey system is also avoided.

ONLINE COMPUTER LIBRARY CENTER (OCLC)
6565 Frantz Rd.
Dublin, OH 43017
(614) 764-6000

The OCLC acquisitions subsystem uses interactive records—records linked so that transactions in one record will automatically cause appropriate changes in others—in several online files to provide current in-process information; constantly updated fund information; periodic, cumulative fund activity and commitment reports; and offline communications to suppliers. Full address and optional predetermined instructions print automatically.

FILES AND FUNCTIONS

When an institution begins to use the subsystem it establishes "background" information for fund records, name-address records and a library control data record prior to creating acquisition records for individual in-process titles

The system will respond only to persons authorized to use the acquisitions subsystem. Authorized operators have been issued passwords. At the start of each session an operator must access the name-address directory, retrieve the organization record with the library control data fields and complete the acquisition-related fields in the record.

Data elements in these fields contain general order instructions to vendors, the sorting sequence for the institution's copies of action forms, the mailing addresses for the fund activity reports and fund commitment registers, the dates for the fund commitment registers, the text of general claim messages and other follow-up information.

Bibliographic Record

The operator searches the online union catalog to retrieve a single bibliographic record that describes the desired item, and to check the holdings and verify that the institution does not already have the item.

When the operator finds the record, the system displays an acquisition workform containing selected bibliographic fields that have been transferred from the online union catalog record. The system transfers the following fields:

Fixed Field Elements		Variable Field Elements	
OCLC #	OCLC number	010	LC card number
Type	Record type	040	Source of cataloging
Bib lvl	Bibliographic level	02X	International standard book number
Freq	Frequency (for serials)	1XX	Main entry
Lang	Language code	245	Title
Repr	Form of reproduction	250	Edition
Enc lvl	Encoding level	26X	Imprint
Mtrl	Type of material (for AV)	30X	Physical description
Ctry	Country of publication	4XX	Series
		7XX	Added entries

The information transferred may be from an order-level (encoding level "O") bibliographic record established by another institution that has ordered the item, or from a cataloging-level bibliographic record (encoding level "I" or "K"). The operator verifies that the bibliographic information corresponds to the desired item and fills in appropriate order fields.

At the top of the acquisition workform, the system supplies a message indicating whether the library has attached its holdings symbol to the bibliographic record, and whether any other library has created an acquisitions record for the item. If this message does not provide sufficient information, a display of the symbols of the institutions that have used the bibliographic record to catalog the item (holdings display request), or those that have created an acquisitions record based on that bibliographic record, can be obtained. This in-process display is useful in developing and supporting cooperative collection development.

If the system does not contain an appropriate bibliographic record, the operator requests an empty acquisition workform and enters bibliographic and order information. The "produce" and "update" commands are then used to create an O-level bibliographic record in the online union catalog. The system assigns an OCLC number to this record and adds it to the online union catalog. Once established in the catalog, an O-level record may be used by other libraries to create acquisitions records. Although O-level bibliographic records are not complete enough to be used for cataloging activities, the system will permit their use for the creation of interlibrary loan requests.

After establishing the bibliographic basis for the order, either using an OCLC record or entering the bibliographic information available, the operator identifies the supplier, bill-to and ship-to addresses, order number (if desired), any further description of the item (e.g., catalog number or subscription information), binding and shipping instructions, verification information, encumbrance amounts, etc.

Acquisitions Record

Once the necessary order information is added to the workform, the OCLC system produces the acquisitions record and also may:

1) Generate offline hard copies (referred to as "action forms") of the order that are sent to the institution, the vendor, or both, depending on the institution's specifications.

2) Enter an O-level record into the online union catalog if the acquisitions record was created from an empty or a "new" workform.

3) Add the institution's three-character symbol to the in-process display of the corresponding bibliographic record.

4) Enter the acquisitions record in the institution's online order file. This "local" record will be updated during the acquisitions process.

5) Adjust fund records based on the amounts encumbered or expended in the acquisitions record.

HELP screens provide an online quick reference guide to the variable order fields in acquisitions records. The operator may consult the HELP screens at any time, including during editing activity. After consulting the screen, the user can return to the acquisitions record without disrupting the editing process.

Often, the same information needs to be recorded on several acquisitions records, perhaps when sending several orders to the same vendor. By using the "constant data" function, repetitive data can be merged into as many acquisitions records as required during one session. The constant data function is terminal specific and remains in place until the operator transfers to another system or logs off.

An acquisitions "save" file is available for temporary storage of acquisitions and fund records. This file, like the cataloging subsystem's save file, may be used to train new users and to review records prior to production or updating. Saved records are retained for seven calendar days, after which the system automatically deletes them from the save file.

The OCLC name-address directory (NAD) is an online file of records that provides complete address information for libraries, associations, processing centers, publishers, vendors, etc. Acquisitions users enter NAD codes in acquisitions records, and the system prints full addresses on offline products. OCLC creates a basic organization record in the name-address directory for each OCLC participant.

Institution-specific data relating to the control of acquisitions processing and the generation of offline products is contained in the library control data fields, which reside in the OCLC participant's NAD organizational record.

An automatic claims component is currently under development. At present, acquisitions users can set the status of an acquisition record to generate a claim or a cancellation notice. Either a standard message or an order-specific message will print on the action form. Users can identify special claim and cancel addresses in the acquisitions record.

Fund Records

Each institution using the acquisitions subsystem can create an unlimited number of online fund records. Each record describes a separate fund or account, based on the institution's financial structure. A fund record identifies the source for the fund and the initial allocation. The system generates the financial activity section of the record, which is displayed as five columns showing the totals of the fund allocation, encumbrances, expenditures, free balance and cash balance. The system constantly updates each category in the current section of the fund record as transactions are posted. At the end of each month a historical activity line is added to the display.

When creating an acquisitions record, the operator identifies the fund record(s) that will be used to pay for the item and also specifies the cost of the item. The system then automatically adjusts the appropriate fund record.

If the system is to encumber and expend automatically, fund records must be created before acquisitions are charged against them. Fund records can be adjusted by authorized operators at any time to reflect credits or transfers. New funds can carry encumbrances or cash balances into a new fiscal period; funds can be closed at any time. Retrieval of fund records is based on the user-supplied fund identification code. This code is the primary identifier for each fund and may be numbers, letters or a combination. A fiscal year qualifier is added to distinguish different years for the same fund.

OCLC offers two types of offline cumulative summary fund reports: the fund commitment register and the fund activity report. OCLC generates and mails reports on microfiche, paper, or both media to the institution. The request to receive these reports and the dates required for periodic cumulations are recorded in the library control data fields.

The fund commitment register is a periodic cumulative report summarizing order activity. It is arranged by fund and subdivided by vendor. Each entry represents one acquisitions record and gives: its order number, date ordered, OCLC number, title, number of copies, bibliographic level, subsequent action dates, encumbrance or expenditure amount, invoice number and date paid (if available) and status of the order. The fund activity report is a cumulative monthly report that shows the financial condition of each online fund.

Receipt Record

When an item ordered through the system is received, the acquisitions record is retrieved by order number or by any of the bibliographic search keys, and the fact of receipt is recorded. The operator then changes the status of the record and updates the record. Automatically, disencumbrances and/or expenditures are posted to the appropriate fund records and encumber field(s) are changed to encumber history field(s).

In addition to recording receipt of materials, vendor reports and invoice processing information, the online acquisitions record also posts credits and generates inquiries to vendors, renewals and reorders, cancellations and claims. Operators enter such information into specific fields and use either the "produce" or "update" command, as appropriate.

Acquisitions records may be created for gifts or items automatically sent to the library through depository programs, exchange or approval plans, or continuation orders. The standard acquisition workform is used to record the relevant order fields. The institution has the choice of whether or not to link this record to a fund record, depending on its policy. If no money is involved, e.g., for a gift or a free publication, only the appropriate bibliographic and order fields are recorded. Such a record will not be linked to a fund record and will not be reflected in offline fund reports. However, to maintain an entry in the offline fund reports for this type of acquisitions record, an institution may choose to create a zero-balance fund record to report titles for which no financial transaction occurs. An institution may choose to control its acquisitions records online, or both online and offline through the fund activity report and the fund commitment register.

When the receiving process has been completed, the status code of the record is changed to "complete" and the acquisitions record enters a limited holding period. The system periodically checks for completed acquisitions records and deletes these records from the files. The order information continues to appear on the fund commitment register through the end of the fiscal year.

RESEARCH LIBRARIES INFORMATION NETWORK (RLIN)
RESEARCH LIBRARIES GROUP (RLG)
Jordan Quadrangle
Stanford, CA 94305
(415) 328-0920

Research Libraries Information Network (RLIN), the bibliographic utility sponsored by the Research Libraries Group, is available to RLG members and to certain other categories of libraries, among them art libraries, law libraries and California Library Authority for Systems and Services (CLASS) libraries.

While the cataloging system has been fully operational for some time, the acquisitions system has until recently been limited to use by Stanford University. The acquisitions software is being rewritten to improve it and to permit its use in a network environment. The acquisitions subsystem is part of RLIN's general online interactive technical processing system, which also supports full authority control and cataloging subsystems in a central integrated system. The RLIN system uses programmable CRT terminals connected to RLIN's mainframe computer on the Stanford University campus. Local printers are housed in the participating libraries to produce forms, reports, etc.

Originally scheduled for implementation in late 1981, the acquisitions system had not been priced by RLG by early 1982. It is generally expected that each acquisitions transaction will cost about the same as a cataloging transaction, with possible additional charges for the printing of some types of forms. This may mean up to $2.50 per title.

Each RLIN library has its own acquisitions processing profile which allows the designation of frequently used data element values (e.g., National Union Catalog codes), processing control and output product selection (e.g., automatic preparation of supplier communications forms without record-by-record instructions), values of locally assigned codes for processing departments within institutions, etc. The profile is available for online input and update to authorized personnel within each user institution.

FILES AND FUNCTIONS

The functions included in the RLIN system are: acquire, upgrade, invoice, fund, codes, print and report.

Acquire

In the acquire function, the operator has full search access to the authorities data base, the cataloging data base and the acquisitions data base. A user's subscription service records and user records in non-acquisitions data bases are available for informational purposes, and bibliographic records from the system-wide data base are available as resource records to be used in building acquisitions records. Authorities data are available for informational purposes only, and may be consulted by the user as appropriate.

Acquisitions data base files available for search-only purposes in this function are: the book fund account file, the requester/selector name and address file, the supplier name and address file. These three files plus the library acquisitions profile and the message file are also used in online work to validate user-input and system-supplied codes or actions.

The acquire function is used to build new in-process file records, to add new acquisitions information to a user's existing in-process file records, or to add acquisitions information to a user's cataloging record for the title.

Record entry in the in-process file of the acquisitions subsystem is performed by use of a pre-formatted, multi-page input screen which presents the user with a combination of prompted control field mnemonics, bibliographic numeric tags, and acquisitions field mnemonics. With economy of notation, the user may record data in the appropriate input screen for later system processing.

In all cases of multiple acquisitions records and/or holding instructions for a title, the system gives the option of displaying to the user all outstanding information for that record at one time.

Indexing and searching are performed according to the general principles of the RLIN technical processing system. Full indexing of bibliographic data in records in the acquisitions subsystem in-process file is performed for data elements such as author, title, control numbers (e.g., the record identification number, the Library of Congress card number) and the like, as well as for acquisitions-specific elements such as supplier invoice number. Online searching can be undertaken through the use of combined indexes and Boolean operators.

A Typical Transaction

A typical transaction in the acquire function might begin when a user performs a data base search for a given title to determine the existence of a resource record and any current order status for the title. The system processes the search against the files in a sequence, which allows the user to determine the status of the title in his own library, and then, if there is no local record, to determine whether there is a resource record for that title. If a resource record is found it may be used as the basis for creating the acquisitions record.

In this case, the user requests the acquisitions input screen and types in the pertinent acquisitions information. An "enter" command instructs the system to edit the coded values and the data elements which must be used in later systems processing control of the record. System diagnosis of errors in the data will be shown on the screen to indicate corrective action. Once the data have been edited, the "enter" command is processed and a record consisting of the bibliographic data and the acquisitions data will be entered into the user's in-process file.

If desired, the completed record can be routed to the user's review file for review and approval the following day. This review process allows confirmation of essential information in the record, the addition of further instructions to the system, revision of work or input performed by new staff, etc., before printing supplier communications forms and internal report forms and before encumbrances are posted against the user's book fund account file. Or, the record can be entered directly into the system, with the required outputs recorded in the user's print queue for local printing and distribution, and encumbrances posted against the book fund account file.

When a user wishes to add a new acquisitions record to a cataloging or acquisitions record already in the data base, the existing record need merely be found in the file—usually in this case through an ID search—and the new acquisitions record added by filling in the information and re-entering the record. The system will respond appropriately to the new entry and will process the information according to the instructions in the acquisitions fields as it would the data in an originally created record.

Record Types

The full spectrum of acquisitions record types is supported by the RLIN system. When a record is created, the user records in the "record type" data element a standard code which instructs the system to treat the record according to the protocols governing that type. For example, if a user is in the acquire function and builds a record containing a code indicating that the title is a gift to the library, the system will not, in reviewing the record for forms processing, prepare a print queue record for a purchase order; in the online system, it will forbid a request for a purchase order.

Certain record type codes are assigned to the variety of continuation orders or extended procurements that libraries place with suppliers and that require special control mechanisms not appropriate to fixed-time orders. These codes are used in system record processing, in online record input and update control, and in output generation.

An example of this special control might be the establishment of a "record level" item structure which treats a set order as a whole, separate from individual items which are anticipated or received on that order. This item structure can be used to claim the extended procurement as a whole without affecting individual items in the record, to cancel the extended procurement with the vendor while still retaining a detailed record of items received, etc.

Material Processing Codes

Working in conjunction with the "record type" data element code are various item-specific material processing control codes. These codes are set by the system either in response to specific user instructions or in response to the series of actions the user has undertaken that trigger an automatic setting of the code. The material processing control codes contribute to record integrity by preventing certain illogical situations from evolving (e.g., force claiming of an item already received), and further contribute to the maintenance of the record's integrity throughout its life.

Based on user-specified requirements in the library acquisitions profile, the system will remove records from the online in-process file and place them in the user's machine-readable archive as they are no longer needed in the online file. The system will also provide a periodic copy of the online in-process file in microform for internal institutional use.

Upgrade

In the upgrade function an institution has full update access to its own in-process file records and search-only access to the authorities file, book fund account file, the user profile, the requester/selector name and address file, and the supplier name and address file. As in the acquire function described above, the account file will be used in online update activity to validate codes, etc., in the record. Access to the bibliographic file is also included, with the same resource record use capability as described above.

Updates may include force claiming a title or item, addition of routing codes designating that the title has been routed to a given processing unit, updating of record status to indicate receipt of material, etc. Here, updates result in a full upgrade of the record to the new status indicated and, in the case of the adjustment of payment information, preparation of data for the invoice report form.

By retrieving the record, frequently through the record identification number, the user will request the appropriate input screen for update. For example, the user may wish to receive an outstanding order in the "material receipt" page of the input screen, input invoice information in the "invoice receipt" page, correct typographic errors in free text fields such as title. Such updating can be done in any combination or singly, as the user desires.

Outstanding in-process file records can also be updated. Any updates to a record's acquisitions information will automatically result in upgrading of affected indexes for the record. Same-day accessibility to the new version of the record will be possible through already existing indexes for the record (new or altered indexes are not available until the next day.)

The upgrade function is also used by restricted accounts for authorization of in-process file records in the user review file. After review, records can be authorized and post-entry system processing performed.

Invoice

The invoice function provides for a detailed summary of supplier invoice information reflected in related in-process file records. In addition, the user may search the in-process file and upgrade fiscal information in the file.

Record entry in the invoice payment file, the book fund account file and the codes and tables is done similarly to in-process file record entry, with various system prompts and economy notation for ease of entry and efficiency of system processing.

Search-only access is provided for the book fund account file, the requester/selector name and address file, the supplier name and address file, and the currency conversion table file. Invoice records are accessible by supplier name and invoice number for local site printing; in the online system invoice records are accessible through the supplier invoice number

In the invoice function, staff prepare and approve for review the RLIN version of the supplier invoice for materials shipped to the institution. The fiscal data recorded in the in-process file record are used as a basis for the invoice report form, which may be additionally notated by the user to reflect invoice level information.

Once an invoice report form has been prepared for approval, the form will be internally reviewed by appropriate library personnel (e.g., accounting personnel or supervisory staff in the acquisitions department) and returned to the operator for online authorization.

The authorization process consists of a simple instruction to the system that an individual invoice has been approved for payment; a record, with date, of this authorization will remain with the invoice report form record for later consultation, if necessary. The authorization of the invoice will cause the disbursement of appropriate funds in the book fund account file overnight.

Invoices can be processed in the system independently of material receipt or following material receipt. The institutional acquisitions profile can be used to specify which practice is desired. If the latter practice is followed, the online system notifies the user if an attempt to process an invoice representing unreceived items is being made.

Fund

The fund function provides search, input and update access to the book fund account file only. No additional file access is provided in this function. The user can add to the book fund account file new codes and names, delete codes and names or modify existing information. The user may set fiscal information pertinent to automated system processing of expenditures against the accounts in the file.

Codes

In the codes function, the user has search, input and update access to the requester/selector name and address file, the locally established supplier name and address file and the coded messages file. In addition, search-only access of the book fund account file is permitted.

Print

The print function provides user access to selected outputs prepared by the acquisitions subsystem for printing at the local site. The user selects the output product to be printed: supplier forms, claim or cancel alert lists, warning lists, invoice payment reports or local report forms for individual titles (e.g., the requester notice). Each day's production is labelled separately in the file. Up to five days output for each of the forms is "saved" or retained in the system.

The user mounts the appropriate form for the output selected and will be able to check alignment against a "forms template" supplied by the system. The printing of the form will start upon command from the user. Each page of the form will be numbered by the system. If the printing is interrupted the user may restart the process by specifying the "page number" at which the printing is to begin.

Report

User requests and specification for management reports are provided through the report function. Though requests for reports can be made at any time, the system will process all users' requests at intervals specified by the system manager. For example, a report request issued on Monday, October 18, 1982 may not be processed until Friday, October 22, 1982.

The system will display the selection criteria available for the report requested and the user specifies data element values to be used in preparing the report and in arranging the data in it.

In all processing, the system provides the control necessary to ensure consistency of processing flow, prevention of unauthorized manipulation of the data and the integrity of relationships of data within the data base (e.g., that invoice amounts can only be charged to existing and valid book fund accounts). Editing of data is performed as they are input online, so that users can make certain corrections immediately. The system gives warning of errors that require supervisor attention before outside communications (e.g., supplier communication forms) are prepared or book fund transactions are made; this warning is given in hard copy form printed locally.

In addition to the online record entry edits, the system provides a full range of textual messages to guide the user through the online system. These messages aid the user in determining the next step to be taken in processing, provide information about search results, diagnose errors that occur in system use or in the application of the institution's profiled intention about system use, etc.

Record processing and indexing is performed through the RLIN overnight process; transactions affecting records in associated files (e.g., an invoice authorization requiring adjustment of balance data in the book fund account file) are also processed overnight.

UNIVERSITY OF TORONTO LIBRARY AUTOMATED SYSTEMS (UTLAS)
130 St. George St.
Toronto, Ontario M5S 1A5, Canada
(416) 978-7171

The Acquisitions and Serials Control (ACS) system of UTLAS (University of Toronto Library Automated Systems) employs a "maxi/mini" approach which attempts to integrate and maximize the benefits derived from both large centralized networks and local autonomous systems. In order to increase the possibility of finding on-order information, cataloging data or interlibrary loan information, a library must have access to a very large data base. On the other hand, for local functions such as online catalog inquiries, circulation control, acquisitions and serials control, the library needs to access only its own holdings or the holdings of a local group of libraries. UTLAS assumes that if large scale automation is to be effective and manageable, large network and local automation activities must be integrated in a cost-effective and efficient way. The "maxi/mini" approach is a form of distributed processing which provides much greater local control than does the typical distributed processing system.

The acquisitions system is still in the development stage, with the ordering module scheduled for completion first. In early 1982 the ordering function was available on a trial basis in a handful of libraries. The system will be implemented in three stages: (1) ordering, (2) receiving and (3) accounting, serials control and inventory control. All types of library materials will be accommodated in this system. User costs are expected to be similar to those of U.S. systems—approximately $2.00 per title.

FILES AND FUNCTIONS

The basic files to be used are: bibliographic file, order file, order sequence number file, customer file, vendor file, vendor purchase order number file, last purchase order number file, invoice control file and fund accounting file. The sub-files to supplement the basic files include user profile and the system profile.

The functions to be permitted through the system are: pre-order searching, ordering, receiving, invoice control, fund accounting, claiming, cancelling, serials check in, renewing subscriptions, binding, routing and management of statistical information.

The access points are ISBN/ISSN, LC card number, precise title, browsable author/title, vendor, purchase order number, publisher and fund. The acquisitions and fund information are accessible only to authorized personnel of the library and authorization is determined by the institution.

Products from the system that can be tailored to the requirement of the library include: purchase orders in a format compatible with the vendor operation, claim notices, cancellation notices, vendor performance reports, fund reports, scheduled and on-demand statistical and management reports, and serials holdings lists.

The latest thinking at UTLAS is that local accounting information will be an essential feature of the acquisitions system. The staff has concluded that many libraries will be unwilling to use a system if it does not have complete confidentiality of local records. To accomplish this, UTLAS plans to use a microprocessor for local fund accounting; the processor will have access to bibliographic records in the UTLAS mainframe computers. Fund accounting could also be accomplished by using an in-house minicomputer that also performs circulation control and other local functions.

WASHINGTON LIBRARY NETWORK (WLN)
Washington State Library
Olympia, WA 98504
(206) 753-5590

WLN is a regional bibliographic utility serving the Northwestern United States and Western Canada. It does not seek members outside its region, but has sold its software to libraries and library consortia throughout the world. The cost of the software depends on what components are purchased, but it is normally in excess of $100,000. The software was originally written for use on an IBM mainframe computer, but it is being rewritten by Burroughs to run on its large systems. The Burroughs-based system is being tested by the Southeastern Library Network (SOLINET).

As of early 1982 the costs for libraries using the WLN system were $3500 for the basic terminal, $2500 for the modem (which accommodates up to 10 terminals) and a service charge of approximately $2.00 per order. Of this charge, $1.15 is for online costs and the remainder is for various optional products which are available at stated costs. Libraries are billed monthly.

As of early 1982, 23 libraries were using the acquisitions system. All are located in the Northwest, with the exception of four libraries in Arizona and Alaska. WLN has determined that libraries acquiring 3000 to 5000 titles per year can accomplish both acquisitions and cataloging functions on a single Hazeltine Modular 1 terminal.

The WLN staff provides two full days of on-site training for library staff and provides extensive customer service backup by telephone. An acquisitions reference manual is also distributed to participating libraries.

A turnkey version of the WLN software with associated stand-alone hardware is available from Biblio-Techniques, Inc. of Olympia, WA. The minimum price is $700,000.

FILES AND FUNCTIONS

The WLN acquisitions subsystem consists of an in-process file, a standing orders file, a name and address file, an account status file and a history file. The first four are online and the history file is maintained on magnetic tape. The bibliographic portion of the records that comprise these files comes from WLN's shared bibliographic subsystem. They are sorted by institution.

The in-process and standing orders files are accessible by purchase order number and by all bibliographic file search keys, including author, title, subject, series, LC card number and ISBN/ISSN. The standing orders file also holds an online payments history.

The name and address file contains names and addresses of vendors, publishers, libraries and branches. It is accessible by the vendor ID number, mnemonic, library ID number or NUC symbol. The account status file maintains accounts and balances for an unlimited number of accounts per library. It is indexed by account number.

When order records are stripped from the online file and placed on magnetic tape, the new file is known as the history file. This is the library's archival copy of its in-process file. If they wish, libraries can receive the history file on microfiche, arranged by purchase order number with a title index.

The online acquisitions records for the WLN system are created and maintained by the library using a series of formatted screens or individual commands. There is some automatic maintenance by the system (checking and alerting for errors) including the production of several batch reports, such as claim letters, and an "exceptional conditions" report.

Each record in the system consists of bibliographic information which is copied automatically from the bibliographic subsystem, fund accounting information, location information and a variety of fixed field information. Once a record is in the system, one can retrieve parts of it by location, accounting data, record status, fixed fields and bibliographic information—separately or all at once.

Access to the system is authorized by password control. Output consists of: purchase order forms, processing of routing slips, vendor report card, notification card for users, claim letters, list of in-process file or standing order file records in title order or purchase order number, exceptional conditions reports and numerous other accounting and management reports.

Special characteristics of the system include a data transmission rate of 4800 baud, two-screened memory buffer, use of a number of formatted screens, and the maintenance of serial acquisitions, including an online payment history. The system performs a great deal of online updating as well as some batch updating.

BAKER & TAYLOR CO.
1515 Broadway
New York, NY 10036
(212) 730-7650

LIBRIS, the online ordering system of Baker and Taylor, and BATAB, the company's batch order and accounting system, have been redesigned and combined to become LIBRIS II, a comprehensive online acquisitions system.

The reports and records produced by this system include: selection lists of new books or specialized bibliographies; purchase orders grouped by vendor and sorted for mailing to vendors; order record cards for each title ordered; open order reports, cumulative lists of titles ordered, not received and recently received, updated weekly; claim notices produced when books have not been received; fund status reports giving current figures on budgets, grants, gifts and endowments; book history providing an acquisitions record in book title detail; and statistical reports as required by the library.

Online fund accounting will be the most significant new component of LIBRIS II. The company scheduled the first demonstrations of the new system for mid-1982.

There were about 30 users of the LIBRIS online order system in early 1982 and three libraries were using optionally produced machine-readable acquisitions records as a source of input for other in-house automated systems. The LIBRIS II system was expected to use an ordering data base of 600,000 titles. These are internal Baker & Taylor records enriched with LC MARC records. With the new approval interface, any user will be able to find out what will be sent on approval. In addition to online fund accounting, the company plans to add open order control and online invoicing. A library will be able to call up an invoice, verify it and automatically apply all amounts to the library's bill from Baker & Taylor. The machine-readable records of all transactions may be used for processing, for invoices or for feeding records into a computerized circulation system.

The price of LIBRIS II is expected to be $1000 or more per month, depending on the library's level of activity. In 1981, using the old LIBRIS online ordering system, most customers were paying less than $1000 per month.

FILES AND FUNCTIONS

The LIBRIS II online acquisitions system is intended to simplify, integrate and improve the library acquisitions process. Basic functions incorporated in the LIBRIS II system are: pre-order searching, online ordering/claiming/cancellation, duplicate order checking, open order control, fund accounting, vendor performance analysis and a cataloging/circulation system interface.

Pre-order Searching

The LIBRIS II data base has been created from Baker & Taylor's internal files, approval and continuation service files, and enriched by external sources, including the Library of Congress' MARC files. All new titles and updates to existing data base records are reviewed by staff before they are added to the data base. Each data base record is checked for completeness and accuracy; for example, the average record includes title, author, publisher, latest price, date of publication, ISBN, ISSN and series name (where applicable), Dewey and Library of Congress Call Numbers, and the latest publisher's status reports.

Libraries access this data base — which is maintained at American Management Systems (Arlington, VA) — through Tymnet or Telenet, via a dedicated computer terminal. Baker & Taylor provides VIP 7800 Series terminals, and PRU 1005 printers. The library arranges for the installation of the Bell Dataphone 2400 service which provides high-speed communications at 2400 bits per second using a dial-up telephone connection. As an option, telecommunication capability of 1200 bits per second—compatible with time sharing services—is provided.

Ordering

The LIBRIS II ordering function is used for pre-order searching, order creation and the placement of orders with suppliers. Titles are searched against the data base on which records may be accessed by ISBN, title, author, title/author and LC card number. As an order is created, multi-copy forms may be generated for internal use or for placing orders through other suppliers. Baker & Taylor orders are transmitted electronically to a regional distribution center, eliminating the cost and delay associated with the mails. In addition, the ordering subsystem allows the retrieval and modification of unreleased orders.

Open order records are created immediately upon release of an order and can be accessed at any time, either prior to or following order fulfillment.

All order records are maintained on the open order file and can be accessed to record subsequent activities including receipts, cancellations and claims. The time retention interval is determined by the library and the open order records remain on the open order file until the designated interval is reached.

Duplicate Order Checking

As orders are placed for a title the system instantly checks all previous orders to determine if that specific title has already been ordered. If duplicate orders are found, LIBRIS II can display a warning message and show details of all previous orders for that title. Upon review, the library may continue with placing the order or undertake additional searches. Duplicate order checking is performed on all titles previously ordered, including both released and unreleased orders.

Open Order Control

The LIBRIS II online acquisitions system enables a library to access the open order file to retrieve an order record or all records on a given purchase order by entering the purchase order number and/or any of the following: ISBN, LCCN, title and title/author. The result of this inquiry is a display of the relevant bibliographic information and the status of the order record.

LIBRIS II provides the ability to modify the quantity or cancel an order within the system even after its release. The system will produce a 3x5-inch multi-copy form which may be used to notify the vendor to amend the original released order. The same capability can be used to accompany books being returned for replacement or credit. The library can request complete open order reports, which are printed on a regular basis in an offline mode.

At a specified interval, LIBRIS II will produce a "claim candidate report" generated by an offline review of the open order file. This report compares the current date with the open order date plus the claim interval as designated on each record. A library may review this report online and access the open order records to create the claim notice and/or record. A library may change the claim interval to have an item appear on the candidate list at some future time.

Machine-readable records are created for Baker & Taylor orders and are electronically transmitted to a distribution center for fulfillment. Claim or cancellation notices are produced for mailing to other vendors and, at the library's option, may also be produced for Baker & Taylor orders.

The system has the ability to cancel all items within a particular purchase order, eliminating the need to retrieve, review and enter data for each item on the order.

Fund Accounting

LIBRIS II retains all fund figures for the prior and current year and allows creation of the new fiscal year's budget online. A library has the option of automatically applying receipts against the prior or current fiscal year based upon the original order date, or of specifying the fiscal period to which each item should be applied. Adjustments to or transfers within the current fiscal budget may also be made at any time.

The system provides security controls, so only authorized library personnel can access the fund accounting files.

As each title is released on order, fund availability is verified and a display warns if the list price of the order exceeds the available dollar balance. An authorized operator may send out an order that exceeds this balance.

As receipts are applied to the open order file the designated fund is automatically reduced by the net price on the invoice. For Baker & Taylor orders, machine-readable invoice records are generated which can be retrieved online and applied by the library.

Online fund sumary reports may be displayed on request, showing the up-to-date balance of a specific fund or group of funds on a summary basis including the last orders released. The displays include the original budget, adjusted budget, amount encumbered, amount expended and available balance. A full printed fund status summary report is sent to the library on a regularly scheduled basis. A library may also elect to receive offline reports showing the detailed make-up of all encumbrances and expenditures applied since the last report.

Vendor Evaluation

On a scheduled basis, the system provides a library with information by which the relative performance of vendors can be evaluated. Report information includes percentage of fulfillment within specified time frames (30, 60, 90, 120, over 120 days), average prices and discounts and average number of days between order placement and receipt.

The data comprising these reports are cumulative from the beginning of a library's fiscal year to date, as determined by a preset parameter for fund accounting maintained as part of the account profile.

BRODART INDUSTRIES
1609 Memorial Ave.
Williamsport, PA 17701
(717) 326-2461

The Brodart On-line Acquisitions System (OLAS) is a modular system that attempts to appeal to a wide variety of types and sizes of libraries. Basically, three systems are offered—OLAS, OLAS II and Book Express Plus.

FILES AND FUNCTIONS

OLAS is an online acquisitions system which uses a Beehive 500 "intelligent" terminal. The features that can be selected are branch ordering, on-order status checking, cataloging and processing, machine-readable bibliographic records, multiple copy order forms and fund accounting. There were 24 customers of the OLAS system in early 1982, including William Patterson College, Buffalo and Erie County Public Libraries, and Arlington County (VA) Public Library.

OLAS II is not as sophisticated as OLAS in that it operates using a "dumb" terminal. With less flexibility, but at a lower cost, smaller libraries are able to order online. There were approximately 50 of these systems in use in early 1982.

The Book Express Plus system provides online access to the title file and warehouse inventory of Brodart. Books in stock are immediately reserved for the ordering library and shipped within 24 hours. Approximately 200 libraries were using this system in early 1982, including some OLAS users. Book Express is a quick, convenient way in which to acquire materials from Brodart's inventory, but the system lacks much of the flexibility of the OLAS system. It is an ordering system that includes fund accounting and on-order files, but does not generate reports or forms.

All three systems have the ability to access the data base of more than 850,000 English language monographs distributed in the United States through normal trade channels. The data base has been built over the last 20 years, based on the demand buying of all types of libraries. In addition to titles listed in *Books in Print* and *Forthcoming Books in Print,* the data base includes out-of-print titles that continue to be in demand by libraries.

Each data base entry includes the author's last name and first initial, title, current U.S. list price, publisher, binding, year of publication, LC card number and ISBN.

All systems offer the ability to place orders online to Brodart. One OLAS program function includes the status of the Brodart warehouse inventory in addition to the title citation. This field is accessible through inventory control account numbers.

Those libraries using the B-500 intelligent terminal are provided with an on-screen form, enabling them to create temporary records on the data base for titles they are unable to find. Copies of a single title for branches of the library can be ordered through the system. A printer may be attached to the terminal in the library to print multiple copy order forms.

The on-order file maintenance function allows for on-order status checking and receiving, and claiming. The fund accounting function allows for encumbrances and expenditures to be recorded online.

OLAS will not only maintain a library's on-order file, but will simplify maintenance by preventing orders for unavailable books. As a result, on-order files will more accurately reflect titles the library can be assured of receiving.

INSTALLATION AND PRICING

Brodart personnel install the equipment and train designated library personnel. The minimum installation commitment is for six months, followed by a ninety-day cancellation option. The library is responsible for providing floor space for the terminal and operator, a temperature and humidity environment similar to a normal household, a 15 AMP, 110V, AC electrical circuit and a telephone line for placing calls to the nearest OLAS network port.

The OLAS system is available on a monthly-fee basis. In 1981 the monthly charge of $985 covered costs for the terminal, printer, network communications and use of the computer time. There are no additional charges for "connect time," "transaction fees," "log on" or "CPU cycles." The cost of the multiple copy order forms and the telephone line to the nearest communication port is assumed by the subscribing library.

Brodart is in the process of revising the pricing structure for the OLAS systems. Information on new prices was not available at the time of publication, although one public library had been informed that prices would go up substantially. There was also evidence that the company was reducing its marketing effort while the reassessment was occurring.

EVALUATION

OLAS is the oldest of the online ordering systems and one of the two oldest onlines acquisitions systems (the other is WLN). It was therefore possible to survey users who had had substantial experience with the system. The author telephoned a number of libraries that had used the system for at least three years.

Most libraries reported that they are anxious to make the system they have installed work, because the concept seems to be such a good one. Frequent operational difficulties were reported, however. The most significant factor contributing to dissatisfaction is the system's transmission. The Brodart supplied terminals and modems operate at 300 baud, and for most libraries this slow speed greatly reduces the efficiency of the acquisitions department. Some libraries have arranged for modems through a local telephone company and have reset the terminals to achieve a 1200 baud transmission rate. Other libraries reported difficulty in adapting to the procedures prescribed by Brodart. While most librarians indicated a willingness to continue to experiment with the system, some felt that it had been faster to acquire materials under their manual system prior to the installation of the Brodart system.

8

Planning and Implementation

The key to the success of any automation effort is planning. The process can vary from an informal discussion among staff to a more lengthy procedure that results in the preparation of a formal written report. Planning in the mind only is still planning, although it is all too easy to overlook an important step when there is no written documentation.

STEPS IN THE PLANNING PROCESS

The steps in problem analysis, long part of management decision making, were concisely adapted to library needs by Taylor and Hiebler[1] more than a decade ago:

1) DEFINE the library's *problem*, including its scope, the environment within which it occurs and any constraints limiting possible solutions.

2) ANALYZE the library's *operations* and, in doing so, describe them in detail showing the relationships among the parts.

3) SYNTHESIZE alternate *solutions*. This is the creative part of the process.

4) EVALUATE the *alternatives* according to defined criteria. Cost and service effectiveness enter in at this point.

5) ITERATE these steps to increase the detail and to modify the results if they do not adequately solve the problem.

The process may be repeated more than once, first in an initial planning study and subsequently in a detailed systems design.

Defining the Problem

The library administration should spell out the purpose of the project, its scope, the amount of time available, the budget and who is to be responsible. Often a committee is given the responsibility but some expert advice will be needed at this stage. An in-house systems analyst or an external consultant can provide some guidance as to what is feasible and the time required to achieve results. The analyst or consultant can also be charged with writing the problem definition. However, if a draft is written by someone who has limited training in systems analysis, it should be subjected to a critique by an analyst or consultant. Key library staff should be involved in extensive discussion of the draft so that errors can be corrected and differences of opinion reconciled. If broad support is achieved early in the project, the prospects for cooperation later on—when the inevitable implementation problems occur—are improved.

Management commitment—both financial and personal—is essential, and should be sought again whenever there is a significant change in the direction or scope of planning. The library administration should be particularly careful to repeat the review of this step with new presidents, provosts, library boards or superintendents who may be appointed during the life of the project. Commitments are both personal and institutional, and the latter are often shaped by the former. It is important to stress at this stage that approval is being sought not to automate, but to address an identified problem. The problem could be reducing high costs, improving inadequate service, records control, or a combination of these.

As soon as approval has been secured, the library administration should appoint a senior staff member as project coordinator. The person must have the time to do the job properly. It is more important that the individual have a good management record than that he or she know a great deal about the specific library activities to be reviewed; information can be acquired more quickly than can good management skills and attitudes.

Analyzing Operations

The next task is to analyze the library's operations. It is this step that is usually cut short by those who are already convinced that the present manual procedures are not working and that automation is the answer. The lack of detailed information about manual operations is also responsible for the lack of cost comparisons between manual and automated library systems. One must be careful to identify the problem, not the symptoms.

For example, a library with a manual acquisitions system was retyping all of the 3 x 5 inch multi-part forms onto state-mandated 8½ x 11 inch purchase orders, and wanted to automate to eliminate the double keying. A consultant quickly saw another way to resolve the problem: The library could issue an 8½ x 11 inch purchase order to both the accounting department and to several hundred vendors at the beginning of the fiscal year. It could then issue sub-orders in 3 x 5 inch format to the vendor only, ordering against the same order number, as needed throughout the year. This procedure would reduce the number of 8½ x 11 inch forms by more than 90%.

The library literature is full of articles detailing techniques for the analysis of library automation and costs, but there have been very few cost studies. Ohio State University undertook a pilot cost study, which documented an increase from a "basic unit cost" per title for cataloging from $8.30 in 1970 to $11.11 in 1975, after implementing OCLC shared cataloging. However, in real dollars, or dollars adjusted for inflation, that would be a decrease of 40 cents from 1970 to 1975.[2] No full-fledged study has yet been published that would provide detailed, reliable cost information about acquisitions and automation.

The price for a good cost study can be very high—up to $10,000 for a whole library and up to $3000 for the study of a single function. There is no point in undertaking a cost study if the decision to proceed is going to be substantially based on other factors, such as service improvements or the availability of better management information. A library may use generalized data, rather than data drawn from an analysis of its own specific operations. The *Annual Review of Information Science and Technology* is an excellent source for up-to-date bibliographies in this area.[3]

Synthesis

The examination of alternatives quickly reveals options that go beyond the automation of existing activities. It is not just a matter of performing the same tasks more quickly or economically. Significant service and management improvements can be realized. An acquisitions system, especially when linked with a circulation system, can become a powerful public service tool by making it possible to request holds against material on order. The statistics can become vital management information for vendor selection.

At this point the library should go back to step one. It is likely that the original problem definition was not formulated in terms as broad as the available options allow. The advantage of a formal, systematic planning process at this point is that it may keep a library from rushing ahead without reexamining the first step. Successful planning is more likely if the library administration and the project coordinator keep the process clearly in mind and are not overwhelmed by pages of reports.

It is the library administrator who must decide, in consultation with higher management and the library staff, whether to adhere to the problem statement as it was first formulated, or to curtail or expand it.

The most common example of this situation occurs when a library administration has authorized planning for an improved acquisitions system and is told that some of the vendors of turnkey online systems offer low-cost microcomputer-based acquisitions systems, while other vendors offer more costly, larger CPU systems that are designed to be integrated library systems. The budgetary constraints and current needs may suggest adherence to the initial plan, but a repetition of the first step of definition may result in a longer-term view and a broader mandate to plan for an integrated system that may better meet the long-term needs of the library.

Evaluation and Iteration

At this stage the library should develop detailed criteria or specifications, against which it will evaluate all alternative solutions. The criteria should outline expected performance, rather than specific methods. The library should prepare its own specifications, rather than rely on a consultant's report or a document received from another library. The participation of several people in the preparation and/or review of the specifications also encourages the interest and commitment of those who will have to operate the system after it is installed. Although more time consuming, this is the surest way to accurately reflect the needs of the library, and to get the interest and commitment of the staff who must later work with the automated system.

Evaluation of vendors' responses will be aided if the specification elements are weighted or grouped into "must," "highly desirable" and "acceptable-if-reasonable" categories. Again, these priorities should reflect the decisions made during problem definition. If they do not, the first step should be repeated.

Once the decision is made to automate, the system must be procured. The normal process is the release of a specification as part of a request for quotation or request for proposal.

THE ROLE OF CONSULTANTS

A consultant can play an important role in assisting a library to acquire the most appropriate automated system to meet its needs. The consultant can advise and assist the library with needs analysis, exploration of options, development of system specifications, evaluation of bids, contract negotiations and the implementation phases of the process.

The amount of responsibility and degree of involvement of the consultant is entirely at the discretion of the library. As a minimal involvement, the consultant can comment upon the process and the adequacy of the documents prepared to date. The other extreme is one of total involvement, with the consultant doing the needs assessment, writing the specifications, evaluating the bids and participating in negotiations.

As with any system vendor, the contract with the consultant is very important. The contract should be explicit about both the degree of consultant involvement and the timing and nature of reports and specifications to be delivered. Should this prove impractical, a mutually agreeable level of effort should be described, either as a part of the contract or in a memo of understanding between the library and the consultant.

In selecting a consultant, the library should determine that the consultant is knowledgeable in library procedures, is familiar with data processing capabilities and limitations, and has some experience in providing consulting to a comparable library.

PERFORMANCE SPECIFICATIONS

Performance specifications need not be detailed nuts-and-bolts statements that spell out how the system should be designed. A performance specification that outlines what the system must be capable of doing is preferable. It usually assures competitive bidding, if that is what is wanted, because there is greater similarity in the capabilities of various systems than in their hardware/software design.

A performance specification may not protect a library against a system design that lacks flexibility for future growth or modification. For a turnkey system the library should specify the minimum size of the central processing unit (CPU), or include in the performance specifications the need for future capability to handle a larger number of terminals and increased secondary storage without replacing the CPU.

Vendors of automated library systems have observed that:

> . . . Libraries do not mean what they say in their specifications. A check of more than a dozen recent contract awards confirms that the lowest bidder is successful far more often than the firm which bids the specifications exactly. A library is usually prepared to sacrifice some features it considers attractive, but not essential, to save a few thousand dollars.[4]

Libraries should decide which features are mandatory before seeking responses from vendors. The mandatory elements can be identified in the specification or retained as a checklist. In either case, the library should plan to abide by its criteria. Some libraries have developed weighted criteria to assist them in evaluating bid responses. Specifications are useful even when dealing with a bibliographic utility that will not participate in a competitive bidding process because the criteria can be used to assess the utility's degree of compliance with a library's needs.

RFQs AND RFPs

The difference between a request for quotation (RFQ) and a request for proposal (RFP) is critical. "Quotations" are normally received when detailed and precise specifications for the desired product are known. The intent is to have the vendor provide a system that meets the library's needs exactly. In such a case the decision-making process ensures that each vendor meets or exceeds all of the specifications and awards the contract to the low bidder.

The "proposal" process recognizes that the evaluation of competing complex products, such as automated library systems, is troublesome and difficult, since any one vendor will usually be able to meet some but not all of the specifications. An RFP involves an evaluation procedure to select the vendor that is most responsive not only in terms of price, but also in degree of compliance to the specifications, delivery date, future support and past performance. For libraries the great advantage of the proposal process is that it enables the selection of a standard system rather than compelling the design of a custom system. Most libraries, therefore, use RFPs rather than RFQs.

The RFP document provides all vendors with general information about the library and its specific needs for the desired system. The RFP generally contains two types of information: first, a listing of the conditions governing the procurement, including instructions for preparing and submitting bids; and second, the functional specifications of the desired system. These functional specifications are developed earlier in the procurement process and should include mandatory requirements as well as optional but desirable features of the system. The RFP process is used to offer all potential vendors an equal opportunity to respond, to obtain for the library the best possible price and to facilitate the evaluation of proposals.

Generally the vendors should be given the opportunity to raise questions, either orally in a vendor's conference and/or by submitting written questions about the RFP. Written responses to all questions are recommended so that all vendors are on an equal footing. Six to eight weeks are generally allowed for vendors to prepare their proposals. Vendors should be required to submit proposals in a uniform format, to assist the library in evaluating the competing products. If such a uniform format is not required, the evaluation process can be very complicated.

In addition to the specifications, vendors are usually provided with information about the relative importance of various functions or features of the desired system, along with a general explanation of the evaluation process that will be used.

The library should either prepare the RFP itself or obtain neutral assistance from a consultant. A consultant can also play an important role in reviewing and critiquing an RFP prepared by the library staff before it is issued to vendors. Such a review can identify inconsistencies and elements that may have been overlooked.

In obtaining responses to the RFP, financial data should be required as a separate section and should not be reviewed by the people doing the evaluation until after the technical review of all proposals has been completed. This will prevent financial judgments from biasing technical considerations. The evaluation of proposals is covered in more detail in the next section of this chapter.

Bibliographic utilities and book wholesalers normally will not respond to RFPs because they do not bid competitively. However, they will respond to specifications sent to them with a request for information about capabilities and price estimates.

EVALUATING PROPOSALS

The first step of an evaluation is to determine the vendor's ability to satisfy the mandatory requirements. If any vendor fails to satisfy those mandatory requirements its proposal is removed from further consideration. All too often none of the vendors are able to meet the mandatory requirements in specifications prepared by library staff. When this happens, it is usually attributable to a failure to study the available systems prior to writing the specifications. Rewriting and rebidding may then be necessary.

After determining which vendors meet the mandatory requirements, the library assesses the degree to which each meets the desirable features or "other system requirements" (items sought by the library unless they are too costly). These other system requirements, though desirable, are items that can be obtained from other sources, accomplished in-house or be done without. In all cases the failure of the vendor to supply the desirable features indicates an additional expense for the library, which has to compensate for the absence of the feature. If the vendor does not offer the desired item or is able only to partially fulfill the requirement for that item, the value or a proportional value of that item should be assessed against the vendor's proposal as a cost item.

The financial review is the last step. In addition to costs provided by the vendor, including bid prices for equipment and software, other cost components must be considered. Five-year costs should be the basis for making the calculations. These can be based on the best available estimates or on the experiences of a number of other libraries. Thus, the request for proposal should require that each vendor submit the name, address and telephone number of a contact person in each library in which the vendor has a system operating. Several people should be interviewed in each library, including the director, the systems specialist and the head of acquisitions.

CONTRACTS

The contract between the library and the automated system vendor is one of the most important and least understood legal agreements signed by a library. In actuality there may be two or more contracts between the library and the vendor, such as one for the procurement of the automated system hardware and software and one for the maintenance agreement. Yet, because of the relative inexperience of librarians in acquiring automated systems, a library may focus on the former and overlook the latter.

Standard vendor contracts for purchase, lease or maintenance are too often viewed as inviolate. In fact, vendor representatives sometimes give the impression that the library must sign the standard contract. On the contrary, whole sections of the contract can be changed or deleted, or new sections added, without invalidating the entire contract. Standard contracts are designed to protect the vendor's interests, not the library's, and important sections can be vague, ambiguous or open to a preferred interpretation. Standard contracts should never be accepted without amendments for the library's protection.

Another impediment to a clear understanding of a contract is the legal terminology often used in writing contracts. It is difficult for librarians to rewrite elements of a contract if they are unaccustomed to using legal expressions, but a librarian can spell out the requirements or intent of the section and let a legal expert translate these items into the appropriate language.

As with any agreement, the contract is intended to formalize the various agreements between the two parties. The contract should reflect its purpose; that is, if reliability (up-time) of system operation is the primary concern, clauses relating to maintenance and support requirements are critical. If response time is deemed the most important objective, emphasis should be given accordingly. Some purchasing policies and procedures may preclude any kind of negotiation, so leverage must be built into the RFP at the beginning. Librarians should either have their agreements reviewed by a lawyer with experience and expertise in the computer contract area, or have their lawyer become more knowledgeable about computer contracts. An extra protection for the library is to have the contract reviewed in draft form by an experienced consultant. The cost for this service may be nominal, and the increased protection for the library can be of substantial benefit if the contract is clarified before difficulties are encountered.

Site Preparation

Site preparation is usually the responsibility of the library, and should begin as soon as the contract is signed. It is a good idea to obtain detailed, written site requirements from the vendor during the negotiation process, and to seek a guarantee that a site meeting the characteristics outlined will be acceptable to the vendor. Any future site modifications necessitated by vendor error, or by a change in the hardware requirements, should be identified as the responsibility of the vendor.

Payment

The terms of payment should be included in the contract. A vendor wants a substantial payment upon signing, because up to 40% of the cost of the contract may represent hardware the vendor has to purchase from manufacturers some time before delivery and installation. A library should pay 40%-50% by the time all of the hardware has been installed. However, initial payment of substantially more than half the contract price may weaken the future negotiating position of the library. The final payment—to be made on acceptance of the system—should be significant, and certainly more than the 20% common in many contracts.

Acceptance

An acceptance test plan should be included as part of the contract. The acceptance test should be a record of consistent performance of all functions specified and bid, for a period of at least 30 days. One hundred percent performance is rarely achieved, but the CPU should be functioning 98%-99% of the time and the total system should achieve at least a 96%-97% level of performance.

Maintenance

The contract should clearly spell out the terms of the maintenance program, for both hardware and software. Hardware maintenance is usually done by the manufacturer(s), but at least one major turnkey system vendor (CLSI) has sought to perform all hardware maintenance itself. The important questions are: (1) Is the service representative nearby? and (2) Is the service representative backed up by a local stock of parts?

Software maintenance may be limited to remedying any defects that are discovered after acceptance of the system, or it may include software enhancements and improvements that are made in the vendor's standard system. The latter benefits the library by providing a dynamic system that can accommodate the constant improvements in library automation. The vendor also benefits because it has to maintain only one standard system rather than several.

STAFF TRAINING

Preliminary training should occur shortly after the contract is signed, when staff interest and curiosity are usually high. Training has several components. The initial training should consist of a basic orientation to the system, as well as demonstrations of what the system will do and how it will affect both the duties of the staff and service to library users. Good publicity at this stage can play an important role in winning staff acceptance of the new system.

Most initial training in the use of systems is undertaken by vendor representatives. A few libraries have chosen to have a small number of people trained by vendors and to have these people, in turn, train the rest of the staff. Libraries that have done this appear to have better ongoing training programs. Turnover in libraries can be high, especially among student employees in academic libraries. There are almost always a few new people who must be made familiar with the equipment. The author has visited more than 50 libraries with automated systems and observed serious misuse of light pens, CRT terminals and printers because staff were inadequately trained. It is a good idea to designate a particular staff member to train new employees and to retrain the others periodically.

9

Future Concerns

There were many unresolved issues in acquisitions automation in early 1982. All of the vendors were well behind their announced development schedules. As each learned of delays in the development of other systems, it appeared to relax its own efforts. Some vendors admitted that they had reassigned staff from acquisitions development to the maintenance of already-released modules.

Not only were the systems available relatively immature in terms of monographs and other firm order procurement, but automated serials acquisition remained a major question mark. Other issues include the trend to integrated systems, systems sharing, optical character recognition scanning, online ordering and increased use of local storage media as opposed to remote data bases. Moreover, there are nontechnological factors to be considered in any attempt to predict the future of automated acquisitions, or any other form of library automation.

SERIALS CONTROL

Serials often represent a significant portion of a library's collection and may consume half or more of the operating budget. While most automated acquisitions systems can handle processing of back files, they cannot accommodate serials check-in and claiming.

Control Problems

The very nature of serials—that they are issued in successive parts which are bibliographically related to previous and subsequent parts—creates control problems for a library. In the purchase of monographs and most nonprint materials, the process is completed when the item is received and the invoice paid. For serials, the routines of verification, ordering, check-in, claiming and paying are part of a continuing process.

A significant part of the control problem arises from the fact that serials are constantly changing. Title changes are common; so are changes in frequency of publication. Moreover, each year thousands of titles cease publication, merge with another publication or are transferred to another publisher. Patrons and library staff often want to know the extent of the library's serials holdings or whether the latest issue published has been received. Binding records must be maintained.

The basic method of controlling serials in a manual environment is a visible file or Kardex. Each title or copy of a title is tracked on a single card. When the cards are inserted in overlapping envelopes, only titles are visible. A single record should contain all the information for a given title, including when the subscription began, the source, frequency, subscription price, fund to be charged, shelving location, binding information, etc.

The procedures for verifying serials are similar to those used for other types of materials. An important part of the verification process is establishing frequency and price, because these elements determine the types of records to be created and the amount that the library will have to set aside each year.

Most libraries order serials through wholesalers. If the regulations of the parent institution permit, the orders may be placed on an "until-forbidden" basis. The wholesaler may then continue to renew the title until the library cancels it. This can reduce paperwork for the library.

It is in check-in that the different character of serials becomes most critical. The average serial is received 6.25 times a year. Some may come daily, others just once a year. Often the only warning a library has that an issue has been shipped is when the following issue is received. Since many publishers of serials produce only a few copies more than the number of their subscriptions, missing issues must be claimed promptly. Yet a claiming mechanism that is triggered automatically by non-receipt a specified number of days after the anticipated arrival may result in excessive correspondence with a wholesaler or publisher over a title that came off the press a few days late or was caught in the postal system.

Many libraries route serial issues to patrons and staff. The check-in clerk must, therefore, add the routing list to the issue when received. In many organizations the routing list changes constantly as people move or interests change. Currently there is no serials control software package that provides adequate support for the routing function.

What Automation Can—and Can't—Do

An automated serials system can solve some claiming problems, providing the serial is published somewhat regularly. Computerization can also assist with financial accounting, for instance by determining the amount spent for serials in particular subject areas. Computer-printed holdings lists or online data bases are a well-established means of distributing holdings information. Of significant assistance in future years will be CONSER (Conversion of Serials), a cooperative project for building and maintaining an online data base of authenticated serial records.

Serials automation seldom handles the most time-consuming clerical procedures or the more difficult professional decisions related to serials. It doesn't speed the opening of the mail, help decide which items should be considered serials whose receipt must be recorded, arrange a pile in proper order, stamp issues with property stamps and date of receipt, locate volume numberings hidden within issues or disperse materials to the proper locations. It does not insert loose-leaf pages in volumes. It does not make a selection between two good journals or predict which will continue to be published. Nor will it locate the source for an important missing issue. The computer cannot decide whether it is better to catalog volumes separately or as a set.

Nevertheless, automation has been used successfully in handling some aspects of serials work in a number of libraries. Some in-house systems exist and a number of health sciences libraries share a system known as Philsom, developed at Washington University, St. Louis. In early 1982, for most libraries the only viable option was the system offered by a major serials wholesaler or subscription agency, F.W. Faxon Co. Faxon is developing a totally automated Serials Check-In Service for customer use. Remote access, online terminals were made available to a limited number of libraries in 1981 for testing and implementation.

The Check-In Service is designed to handle all current titles received by a library, including titles acquired direct from the publisher, another vendor or by gifts and exchange. The basic record for each title can be viewed on two displays that contain the current check-in information as well as additional details related to claims, replacements, shelving locations, routing and marking instructions, holdings, binding instructions, etc. Previous years' check-in records can be viewed in a third and subsequent displays.

A major feature of Faxon's Serials Check-In Service is its Claims Warning System. Printouts are regularly issued for titles which may need a claiming action because of lapses, gaps or delinquencies. Claims for Faxon-placed titles will be handled by Faxon personnel.

Timely reports are another integral part of the service. A variety of weekly, biweekly and monthly printouts can be obtained both for public service and collection management. As an additional service to serials check-in users, some of Faxon's internal files may be accessed. Bibliographic and financial information, publishers and their titles, as well as the customer's current and retrospective files, will be available to libraries. Member libraries may also be able to view other libraries' check-in files by prior authorization.

INTEGRATED SYSTEMS

It is unlikely that separate single-function systems such as those for serials control will continue to attract libraries when a variety of integrated systems become available. If the turnkey vendors and bibliographic utilities fail to offer attractive circulation control subsystems, there will be a great demand for linking systems with those of other vendors, particularly the in-house systems. Should that happen, libraries will increasingly regard the in-house system as a control center through which they can access a variety of data bases and processing systems. A library might choose to assemble a "hybrid" system with in-house, bibliographic utility, commercial data base service and wholesaler supplied components. While the in-house system might itself be capable of supporting an integrated system, it would be used to connect automated services of several outside sources for reasons of economy and/or the availability of attractive features.

SYSTEMS SHARING

The sharing of systems will continue to be a factor in all areas of library automation, including acquisitions. Minicomputer-based systems are becoming more powerful and more capable of supporting multiple functions for several libraries. Smaller libraries are more frequently deciding to pursue automation, not just because shared systems can be cost effective, but also because they facilitate resource sharing. In early 1982, approximately 250 libraries were sharing systems, almost all of them circulation control systems. A majority of those contacted by the author envisioned sharing other functions on the same computer system.

Some of the acquisitions systems available in early 1982 could not support a shared acquisitions system except as the libraries agreed to order through a single agency or use identical procedures. A consortium or a library that contemplated sharing an acquisitions system, therefore, had to specify that multi-institutional capability would become available within a reasonable period of time. Vendors that lacked the ability to support multiple users were already beginning to feel a softening of their markets. It is likely that within a few years all vendors remaining in the library automation market will offer this capability.

OCR SCANNING

There may be a long-term trend away from bar-code labeling technology to OCR (optical character recognition) symbology, which is both machine- and human-readable. The publishing industry is beginning to record the ISBN on books in OCR form, and libraries are beginning to entertain the idea of scanning the numbers with an OCR wand and matching the identifier scanned against a data base, such as that of a large bibliographic utility or the library's on-order file. Therefore, keying would be eliminated. In fact, one could envision OCR scanning the ISBN from a brochure or other publication announcement so that the order could be formulated without keying bibliographic information. The elimination of keying will not only reduce costs—presently at least $1.95 per 1000 characters keyed—but will also reduce errors in data entry.

ONLINE ORDERING

Online ordering, now offered only by the wholesalers, is likely to become a feature of all systems. What is needed is agreement on protocols. The book industry is actively working on protocol development and OCLC, the largest of the bibliographic utilities, is negotiating with several large vendors to accept online orders from OCLC participants. The typical transmission might include just the quantity, the ISBN and the library's identification code. While online ordering will require greater reliance on telecommunications, the cost will be modest because of the small amount of information transmitted for each order (possibly as few as 20 characters). Orders would be transmitted at the rate of several hundred per hour.

LOCAL STORAGE MEDIA

On the other hand, for accessing bibliographic records (at an average length of 700 characters) the long-term general trend may be away from remote data bases and toward the use of periodically replaced local data bases, as costs for telecommunications continue to increase while costs for storage media continue to go down. It may become practical for bibliographic utilities and wholesalers to supply libraries with bibliographic records and availability information on optical discs or other low-cost storage media that can be accessed with a local computer. There are already optical video discs that can store 12.5 billion characters of information in digital or machine-readable form. If the cost of duplicating optical discs from a master disc drops to $10—as has been predicted—a library could be sent a complete and updated bibliographic file every two weeks for less than the present annual telecommunications costs for linking a terminal to a bibliographic utility. Minimarc, the stand-alone cataloging support system, has already demonstrated the viability of providing this type of service with the less attractive floppy disc medium. Wholesalers could send optical discs listing their inventories to libraries that order more than 10,000 titles a year—approximately 300 libraries and school districts. Only the actual brief online order would then have to be transmitted from the library to the vendor.

NONTECHNOLOGICAL FACTORS

All of these future scenarios are technologically sound, but the future of technology is more dependent on nontechnological factors. The diffusion rate for new technologies is much slower than many forecasters concede. It can be 10 to 20 years from the time that something is technologically feasible until it is in widespread use. There are many constraints on the spread of a new technology: economic factors, marketing priorities, government regulation and personal attitudes.

In the case of automated acquisitions, many vendors may not be able to afford to receive online orders, or to provide libraries with machine-readable records of their inventories. Those who do have the money may decide that their marketing priorities do not emphasize support for library automation. Government regulations may impose a constraint by fixing the cost of telecommunications at a high level, restricting the use of copyrighted bibliographic information or restraining the reformatting of information not previously in machine-readable form. Finally, there may be people—publishers, wholesalers, librarians—who resist automation even though it may be technologically and economically feasible.

Technology will undoubtedly play a growing role in the library of the future. Already the cataloging operations of more than 3000 libraries have been transformed; more than 400 libraries have automated circulation; and nearly 100 libraries had installed an automated acquisitions system by early 1982. While the number of libraries using automated cataloging may not grow to more than 5000, as many as 1000 libraries—a ten-fold increase

—may install integrated automated systems, including acquisitions systems, by the mid-1980s. This is a remarkable growth rate in so short a time. Nevertheless, librarians will continue to make their decisions in the context of their overall needs and resources. Automation will continue to be only a tool for the librarians to achieve their objectives, and not the answer to all problems.

Footnotes

Chapter 1

1. University of Illinois, Chicago Circle, *Annual Report of the Library 1947-48* (Chicago, IL: The Library, 1948).
2. Based on a random sampling undertaken by the author's firm in 1981.
3. Joseph Becker and Robert M. Hayes, *Handbook of Data Processsing for Libraries* (New York: John Wiley & Sons, 1970), p. 109.

Chapter 3

1. *Overview of Computerized Library Networking in Canada* (Ottowa: National Library of Canada, 1979), p. 25.

Chapter 6

1. Rober Wiederkehr, *Alternatives for Future Library Catalogs* (Rockville, MD: King Research, Inc., 1980).

Chapter 8

1. Robert Taylor and Caroline Hiebler, *Manual for the Analysis of Library Systems* (Bethlehem, PA: Lehigh University, 1965).
2. D. Kaye Gapen and Ichiko T. Morita, "A Cost Analysis of Ohio College Library Center On-Line Shared Cataloging System in the Ohio State University Libraries," *Library Resources and Technical Services* (Summer 1977), pp. 286-301.
3. For ideas consult Geoffrey Ford, *Library Automation: Guidelines to Costing* (Wetherby, England: British Library Lending Division, 1973, ED082-757).
4. Richard Boss, "Circulation Systems: The Options," *Library Technology Reports* (January/February 1979), p. 81.

Appendix I: Criteria for Conducting a Cost Study

• *Study current rather than past work.* Measure acquisitions, cataloging or circulation as it is being done. Don't just look up last year's statistics and divide the number of units of work into the total costs. Records not developed for a cost study will rarely be sufficiently detailed and accurate to produce reliable data.

• *Express measurements in time first, then convert into costs.* Costs are constantly changing. Measurements of how long something takes to do will remain useful for some time if costs are updated periodically.

• *Use in-person measurement rather than questionnaires.* People interpret questionnaires differently and define activities differently.

• *Prepare the participants.* The participants must know why the study is being done and must cooperate in achieving the objectives. There is a real danger of a "Hawthorne Effect," or an increase in performance by people who are being watched. Measure as near normal operations as possible, and be prepared to discard the results of the first hour.

• *Distinguish between level of personnel required and level actually performing a task.* Many manual operations are performed by too high a level of personnel. Costs can be altered by changing staff around. The same is true for an automated system. The library must make certain that the comparison of two options is based on similar staffing practices.

• *Break a process into activities.* Don't measure acquisitions as a single process, but break it into the activities of searching, ordering, receiving, paying, etc. The automated process may be less costly for each of these activities, but it may be more costly overall because new activities have been added, such as the generation of management information.

• *Define each activity.* Don't assume that everyone defines an activity the same way. For example, some library staff consider "ordering" to be the preparation of purchase orders, while others consider it as determining the selection of the vendor, which account to use, and the typing of the purchase order.

• *Include all costs, both direct and indirect.* The staff time and order forms used in order preparation are direct costs, but the amortized cost of the furniture and typewriter, the floorspace, the lighting and climate control are all indirect costs, as are the support services of custodians, payroll clerks and mailroom personnel. Supervision is also a significant cost. The training of a clerk who types the orders must also be considered.

• *Adjust for time lost due to illness, accidents, tardiness, idle time, etc.* If for 20% of the year the person is not actually performing his or her duties, the cost of that lost time must be charged to the productive time.

• *Provide for checks on data during the study.* One must check the data periodically to determine that the "Hawthorne Effect" is not occurring and that readings from day to day are not varying dramatically.

Appendix II: Glossary

The following brief definitions are offered for laymen and perhaps lack the precision a specialist might prefer. Only those terms used in this report and those most commonly used in the vendors' general literature are included.

AACR: Anglo-American Cataloging Rules, a widely accepted set of rules for describing and establishing name headings for books and other library materials. The second edition (AACR 2) was published in 1978.

Access time: See *Response time.*

Acquisitions: The area of technical services involved with the acquiring of books, periodicals and other materials by purchase, exchange or gift.

Address: The location in the storage of a computer of a name, number or other data element.

Analog: The representation of values or characters electronically by means of physical variables (variations of electronic pulses). Voice-grade telephone lines are analog, as distinguished from the digital representation used in computer systems.

ANSI: The American National Standards Institute, a body that has established voluntary industry standards for business equipment manufacturers. It has accepted many programming languages as ANSI standards, which can be taken as evidence that they are well established and generally sound. ANSI standard languages used in automated library systems include COBOL, FORTRAN and MUMPS.

Application package: A set of computer programs or software used to solve problems in a particular application.

Approval plan: An agreement between a library and a vendor that all books of a publisher or all volumes fitting certain criteria will automatically be sent, with the library having the option of returning unwanted volumes.

Asynchronous communication: A method of data transmission dependent only on the condition of the transmitting line at that time, and not the condition of the hardware or software at either end.

Author: The person or corporate body chiefly responsible for the intellectual or artistic content of a work, whose name is included in the author file.

Authority file: A record of the "correct" or chosen headings to be used for names, subjects or series. Its purpose is to provide consistency.

Auxiliary storage: See *Secondary storage.*

Background: The execution of lower priority programs at the same time as the higher priority ones but without interfering with them. The other major option is to process the lower priority work overnight.

Bar-coded labels: Machine-readable identification symbols printed on paper strips for attachment to library materials and patron identification cards. Bar code symbols represent binary numbers by using height, width, distance between vertical bars or relationship among bars to express characters. Codabar labels developed by Pitney Bowes and marketed by Monarch are the most widely used in library applications.

Batch processing: Processing of data after it has been accumulated over a period of time, as opposed to processing it immediately or online.

Baud: A unit of signaling speed. One baud most commonly means that one bit moves through a line every second. Common low and high speed baud rates are 300 bits per second (bps) and 1200 bps.

Bit: A unit of information that is the smallest unit in the binary system used in computer systems. A bit is a representation of one or zero. It is the combination of these that represent the data.

Blanket order: An agreement to purchase one or more copies of all books issued by a publisher.

Bug: A malfunction or error.

Byte: A series of bits that constitute a character (a letter or number) most commonly eight bits.

Card punch: A device used to record information on cards by punching holes in them.

Card reader: A device that senses the holes in a punched card and translates these into machine code for the computer.

Central Processing Unit: See *CPU*.

Claim: A follow-up on an order or subscription to determine why a missing item has not arrived.

Command: An instruction given in machine language, such as from a terminal to the computer, to execute a particular program.

Compiler: A computer program used to translate other computer programs (in a high-level language) into machine language.

Composite terminal: One that offers light pen or OCR wand and keyboard functions in one unit.

Conversion: The process of changing from one method of recording and manipulating data to another, e.g., from manual to computerized, or from one computerized system to another.

CPU: Central processing unit, the part of the computer that actually performs the computations.

CRT: A cathode ray tube, used to display information visually; now also called a VDU (visual display unit).

Cursor: A solid underscore that appears under a character or space on a CRT or VDU to show where the next character entered will appear.

Data base: The entire collection of files maintained in the computer system.

Data compression: The reduction of storage space required by eliminating gaps or redundancies not essential to an intelligible record.

Data management: The organizing, locating, storing, maintaining and recovering of data and the programs developed to accomplish that.

Data processing: A sequence of operations that manipulates data according to a previously developed plan.

Data set: See *Modem*.

Debug: To identify, locate, analyze and correct a malfunction or error in a computer.

Dedicated computer: A computer devoted to exclusive use as opposed to one which is shared with other users who maintain different files and may control them differently.

Diagnostic routine: A program that is run periodically to detect malfunctions or errors.

Disk: The principal means of storing information in a computer system. The capacity of disk storage is usually measured in megabytes. See also *Disk pack* and *MB*.

Disk pack: A package containing several individual platters or disks (five or more commonly), each of which has hundreds of tracks of information. The tracks are sub-divided into several dozen sectors. It is these sectors that are "accessed" when entering or reading information.

Distributed processing system: An in-house system that does not stand alone, but relies on a host computer outside the library, or organization, to do part of the processing. The host usually has a greater storage capacity and faster printing capability.

Documentation: The detailed record of decisions made in developing a computerized system that is necessary to replicate, repair or enhance the system.

Down-time: The time during which a system or a part thereof is not functioning.

Dump: To copy from storage, or the actual data from that action. A tape dump is often obtained for back-up or for sending to another library.

Field: Part of a record. The specific area used for a particular category of data such as title, call number.

File: A group of related records such as a vendor file, on-order file, etc.

File layout: The arrangement of the elements of the file including the order and size of the elements.

Fixed-length record: A record that has the length fixed in advance rather than being varied according to the actual extent of the contents. See also *Variable-length record*.

Front-end systems: A form of distributed processing. The computer in a library, usually a micro, is used only for minor processing and the bulk of the work and the files are handled on a host computer.

Function: A specific machine action that may be initiated by a function key or by an internal instruction. A number of predefined functions can be initiated by a terminal operator.

Hard copy: A printed copy of machine output, as opposed to temporary display on a CRT or VDU.

Hardware: All of the tangible components of the computer system, including the central processing unit, disk drives, terminals, etc., as distinguished from the programs that operate the system (software).

Hit: A successful matching of two items. In conversion, one may seek to utilize another library's records by search key to minimize the time and cost of data entry. The hit rate is the percentage of successful matches.

Host computer: The controlling or principal computer in a system that ties two or more computers together.

Housekeeping: Operations that prepare or maintain the computer to do the processing needed by a library.

Index or index search: An index is used to locate the contents of a file together with the pointers to access the data. In an index search, the system matches the search key with an index entry which points to the physical location. If a file is very large, there will be several levels of indexes. The index entries are arranged sequentially; it is, therefore, possible to search by partial keys when one does not have full author or title.

Inquiry: A request for information from storage.

Interface: The linking of two or more computers, or, the accessing of the storage of a computer by two or more computer programs.

Inverted file: A file created from another by altering the sequence of the fields or by creating a cross index to another file so that a key word identifies a record. Call number access often involves inverting a file.

ISBN: International Standard Book Number, a distinctive and unique number assigned to a book. It is hoped that eventually all publishers throughout the world will participate in the system.

ISSN: International Standard Serial Number, a distinctive and unique number assigned to a serial.

In print: Currently available from the publisher.

Jobber: A wholesaler who stocks or supplies the books of many publishers for resale to bookstores and libraries.

K: 1024 bytes. Each byte is a character or number.

KB: Kilobyte. A term used to describe the primary storage capacity of a computer. See also *MB*.

Keyboard: A device for entering data by pressing keys as opposed to badge reading or scanning with a light pen or OCR wand.

Keypunch: A keyboard device that punches holes representing data in cards so that they will be machine-readable.

Language: A set of software representations and rules used to convey information to the computer.

Light pen: The pen-shaped device used to read bar-coded labels.

Line printer: A device that prints all the characters of a line as a unit rather than one character at a time.

Magnetic tape: A tape with a magnetic surface on which machine-readable data can be stored.

Mainframe: A full-sized computer system based on a CPU, the memory of which is normally measured in megabytes.

Main storage: That which is directly accessed as opposed to that which is in auxiliary storage or secondary storage (e.g., on magnetic tape). See also *Storage.*

Maintenance: Any activity to keep computer hardware or software running, including not only repairs, but also tests, adjustments and scheduled replacements.

Management information: The data organized in such a way as to aid in the management of an enterprise. Management information usually consists of statistical cumulations.

MARC: Machine Readable Cataloging, a program of the Library of Congress in which machine-readable cataloging is distributed in LC format.

MB: Megabyte. A term normally used to describe the secondary storage capacity (such as disks) of a computer. Each megabyte is one million characters or numbers.

Memory: Same as storage.

Microprocessor: A complete computer processor on a single integrated-circuit chip approximately the size of a dime.

Microcomputer: A microprocessor with associated input and output capability. Generally distinguishable from a minicomputer by lower price, processing speed and capacity.

Minicomputer: A physically compact digital device that has a central processing unit, at least one input-output device and a primary storage capacity of at least 4000 characters.

Modem: A device that makes computer signals compatible with communications facilities.

Network: A number of communication lines connecting a computer with remote terminals or with other computers.

OCR: Optical character recognition, or, a type font that can be read by both humans and machines. The best known is OCR-A, the type approved by the National Retail Merchants Association. An OCR wand is a device that, when passed over the special type font, "reads" the data into the machine.

Offline: Equipment or storage not under control of the central processing unit.

Online: Equipment or storage under the control of the central processing unit so that a user can interact directly with the computer.

Out of print: No longer available from the publisher.

Password: A symbol a person gives when first beginning to use the system to identify him/her or to gain access to restricted functions.

Periodical: A publication issued in successive parts at stated or regular intervals and intended to be continued indefinitely. Usually it has a distinctive title, each issue contains articles by different contributors, and there are two or more issues per year. Newspapers and society proceedings are generally not considered periodicals, but usage of the term varies from library to library. See also *Serial*.

Peripheral equipment: Anything other than the central processing unit of a computer system that provides the system with external communication.

Pointer: An address or other way of indicating location.

Polling: A technique by which each of the terminals or computers sharing a communications line is queried to get information.

Port: The part of the central processing unit that provides a channel for receiving or sending data from or to a remote device. More than one such device may be put on a port.

Printer: An output device that converts machine code into readable impressions on paper or microform.

Program: A series of instructions for computer actions to perform a task or series of tasks.

Prompting or prompts: A function that tells a terminal user what to do next, or asks what he or she wants to do next.

Queue: A waiting line of data either in the order received or in another order previously determined.

Real-time processing: Provision of data at the time a user is at a terminal so those responses may be used in further queries.

Record: A collection of related items of data treated as a unit. The author, title and call number fields may constitute the item record in a circulation system.

Record length: A measure of the size of a record, usually in characters.

Release: A periodic revision of software that is distributed to all customers of a circulation system vendor.

Response time: The time between the entry of a query and the beginning of the response on the screen, printer or other output device.

Search: To examine a number of items in a file in order to find one or more that meet the characteristics or properties specified by the requester.

Search key: The data entered in (properties specified) for the conducting of the search.

Sequential search: The examination of each item in the order in which the items are arranged on the disk or other storage medium. This method is most suitable for such records as patron names and addresses.

Serial: An inclusive term for publications issued in successive parts at regular or irregular intervals and intended to be continued indefinitely. Includes periodicals, newsletters, proceedings, reports, memoirs, annuals and numbered series.

Simulate: To represent features of the behavior of one system by another; for example using a large computer to simulate the behavior of a minicomputer for the purpose of testing software or the effect of a specific number of terminals.

Software: A set of programs, procedures and documentation concerned with the operation of a computer system.

Stand-alone: A computer system that is capable of performing all the specified functions without the help of another computer, such as is necessary in a distributed processing system.

Standing order: An order for all works in a series, all volumes of a set or all editions of a work.

Storage: The memory of a computer. The device in which data are held for later retrieval and use. See also *Main storage.*

Terminal: A point in the computer system at which data can be entered or withdrawn.

Throughput: The total amount of work a computer system performs in a specified time period.

Time sharing: A method of using a computer system to allow a number of users to execute programs at the same time, with the system servicing them in such rapid sequence that the requests appear to be handled simultaneously.

Truncate: To terminate a process or to shorten fields according to previously established rules.

Turnkey: A complete system provided by a vendor, including equipment, software and training.

Update: To modify a file with current information.

Variable-length record: A file in which the records need not be uniform in length but are only as long as the amount of data warrants.

VDU (visual display unit): See *CRT*.

Selected Bibliography

Alley, B., and Cargill, J.S. "Automated Acquisitions Systems; Or, Does Your Library Acquire Materials Bit by Bit?" *Library Acquisitions* 4 (1980): 113-115.

Automated Acquisitions. Washington, DC: Association of Research Libraries, Office of Management Studies, 1978: SPEC Kit 44.

"Automated Acquisitions Systems: Papers Presented at the LITA Institute." *Journal of Library Automation* 13 (December 1980): 155.

Automated Acquisitions: What's Good? What's Bad? What's Missing? Phonodisc, recorded at American Library Association 97th Annual Conference, Chicago, June 1978. Chicago, IL: American Library Association, 1978.

Automation in Libraries. C.A.C.U.L. [Canadian Association of College and University Libraries] Workshop on Library Automation, University of British Columbia, Vancouver, April 10-12, 1967. Ottawa: Canadian Library Association, 1967: ED 021 583.

Boss, Richard W., and Marcum, Deanna. "On-line Acquisitions Systems for Libraries." *Library Technology Reports* 17 (March/April 1981): 115-202.

Bruer, J.M. "Management Information Aspects of Automated Acquisitions Systems." *Library Resources and Technical Services* 24 (Fall 1980): 339-342.

Buckland, Lawrence F.; Dolby, James; and Madden, Mary. *Survey of Automated Library Systems; Phase I. Final Report.* Maynard, MA; Inforonics, Inc., 1973.

Cargill, J.S. "Online Acquisitions: Use of a Vendor System." *Library Acquisitions* 4 (1980): 236-245.

Clinic on Library Applications of Data Processing. *Proceedings: Applications of Minicomputers to Library and Related Problems,* edited by F. Wilfrid Lancaster. Urbana IL: University of Illinois Graduate School of Library Science, 1974.

Dowlin, K.E. "Fitting the Pieces of the Puzzle Together: Acquisitions." *Library Acquisitions* 4 (1980): 13-18.

Dunlap, Connie R. "Mechanization of Acquisitions Processes." In *Advances in Librarianship,* vol. 1, pp. 35-57. edited by Melvin John Voight. New York: Academic Press, 1970.

Ford, Stephen. *Acquisitions of Library Materials.* Chicago, IL: American Library Association, 1978.

Greenberg, Esther. *Innovative Designs for Acquisitions and Cataloging Departments as a Result of Library Automation.* Cleveland, OH: Case Western Reserve University, School of Library Science, 1974: ED 096 993.

Hayes, Robert M., and Becker, Joseph, *Handbook of Data Processing for Libraries.* New York: John Wiley & Sons, 1970.

International Business Machines Corp., Data Processing Division. *Library Automation, Introduction to Data Processing.* White Plains, NY: IBM, 1972.

Kennedy, James H., and Sokoloski, James S. "Man-machine Considerations of an Operational On-Line University Library Acquisitions System." *Proceedings.* American Society for Information Science, 33rd Annual Meeting, Philadelphia, October 11-15, 1970. Washington, DC: American Society for Information Science, 1970.

Kilgour, Frederick G. "Effects of Computerization on Acquisitions." *Program: News of Computers in Libraries* 3 (November 1969): 95-103.

Kimber, Richard T. *Automation in Libraries, 2nd ed.* Oxford and New York: Pergamon Press, 1974.

LARC Association. *Survey of Automated Activities in the Libraries of the United States. Bibliography of Literature on Planned or Implemented Automated Library Projects.* A Survey of Automated Activities in the Libraries of the World, vol. 1 and vols. 6-9, respectively. Tempe, AZ: LARC Association, 1973.

LARC Institute on Acquisitions Systems and Subsystems. *Proceedings.* Lake Geneva, WI, May 25-26, 1972, edited by H. William Axford. Tempe, AZ: LARC Association, 1973.

Lukac, J. "Evolution of an Online Acquisitions System." *Journal of Library Automation* 14 (June 1981): 100-101.

Madden, Mary A. "Minicomputer Applications in Acquisitions and Cataloging." *Proceedings.* American Society for Information Science, 39th Annual Meeting, San Francisco, October 4-9, 1976. Washington, DC: American Society for Information Science, 1973.

Martin, Susan K., and Butler, Brett, eds. *Library Automation: the State of the Art II.* Papers presented at the Preconference Institute of Library Automation, Las Vegas, June 22-23, 1973. Chicago, IL: American Library Association, 1975.

"Online Serials Check-in Service Designed by Faxon." *Journal of Library Automation* 13 (Summer 1980): 207.

Palmer, Richard. "Library Automation: Getting What You Pay For." *Proceedings*. American Society for Information Science, 36th Annual Meeting, Los Angeles, October 21-25, 1973. Washington, DC: American Society for Information Science, 1973.

Palmer, Richard P. *Case Studies in Library Computer Systems*. Ann Arbor, MI: R.R. Bowker Co., 1973.

Pearson, Karl M., Jr., "Minicomputers in the Library." In *Annual Review of Information Science and Technology,* pp. 139-163. Washington, DC: American Society for Information Science, 1975.

Pemberton, J.E., and Clifton, B.J. "Online Book Ordering in the College Library." *Library Association Record* 83 (January 1981): 15.

Potter, W.G. "Automating Acquisitions in Academic Libraries." *Illinois Libraries* 62 (Summer 1980): 637-639.

Salmon, Stephen R. *Library Automation Systems*. New York: Marcel Dekker, 1975.

Salton, Gerard. *Dynamic Information and Library Processing*. Englewood Cliffs, NJ: Prentice-Hall, 1975.

Schultheiss, Louis A. "Data Processing Aids in Acquisitions Work." *Library Resources and Technical Services* 9 (Winter 1965): 66-72.

Taylor, Gerry M.; Hansard, James W.; and Anderson, James F. "Cut to Fit." *Library Resources and Technical Services* 14 (Winter 1970): 31-35.

Tedd, L.A. *Introduction to Computer-Based Library Systems*. London and New York: Heyden, 1977.

United States Library of Congress, MARC Development Office. *Order Division Automated Systems*. Washington, DC: Library of Congress 1972: ED 077 516.

Veaner, Allen B. "Major Decision Points in Library Automation." *College and Research Libraries* 31 (September 1970): 299-312.

Weber, David C. "Personnel Aspects of Library Automation." *Journal of Library Automation* 4 (March 1971): 27-37.

Index

ABOUT THE AUTHOR

Richard W. Boss is Senior Management Consultant, Information Systems Consultants Inc., Bethesda, MD, and Boston, MA. He has served as a consultant to more than 100 libraries and library consortia on the selection and procurement of automated library systems. In addition, he has been a consultant to three automated acquisitions vendors.

Mr. Boss was formerly University Librarian at Princeton and Director of Libraries at the University of Tennessee at Knoxville. He is the author of *The Library Manager's Guide to Automation* (1979) in Knowledge Industry Publications' Professional Librarian series. His other publications include "Automated Circulation Systems," *Library Technology Reports* (May/June 1982); *Developing Microform Reading Facilities* (Microform Review, 1981); and "Automation and Approval Plans," *Advances in Understanding Approval and Gathering Plans in Academic Libraries* (Western Michigan University, 1970). He is a graduate of the University of Utah and holds an M.A. in Library Science from the University of Washington.